WONDERFUL COUNSELOR

A **GOD** WHO WILL **HELP US**
THROUGH OUR DARKEST TIMES

WONDERFUL COUNSELOR

A **GOD** WHO WILL **HELP US**
THROUGH OUR DARKEST TIMES

DREW YOUNG

CFI
An imprint of Cedar Fort, Inc.
Springville, Utah

Paperback ISBN 13: 978-1-4621-4501-0
Ebook ISBN: 978-1-4621-4651-2

Published by CFI, an imprint of Cedar Fort, Inc.
2373 W. 700 S., Suite 100, Springville, UT 84663
Distributed by Cedar Fort, Inc., www.cedarfort.com

   Library of Congress Registration Number: 2023942339

Cover design by Shawnda Craig
Cover design © 2023 Cedar Fort, Inc.
Edited and typeset by Valene Wood

Printed in the United States of America

10 9 8 7 6 5 4 3 2 1

Printed on acid-free paper

To my mom and dad, Stephanie and David Young.

Thank you for emulating the Savior in my life,
and for teaching me of his love, goodness,
and divine mission to do His Father's will above all else.

Other books by Drew Young:

The Meaning of Your Mission:
Lessons and Principles to Know You Are Enough

Stand Guard at the Door of Your Mind

Contents

Introduction

Sometimes the most difficult trials in our life can make room for the greatest triumphs. Having dealt with varied dark times since I was nearly five years old, I can relate to and have compassion for those who have walked similar paths. For me, treading the path of mental and emotional health challenges has been the instigator for a majority of the difficulties I've experienced during my sojourn on earth. Maybe you can relate . . . or maybe not. Perhaps physical handicaps have challenged you. Maybe it's been a food allergy. Maybe you've struggled with overwhelming shyness, sexual abuse, a failing relationship, a wayward child, or a problematic marriage. Regardless of what instigates our dark times as human beings, the importance of understanding and internalizing the fact that we have a God who "gets it" and will help us through those times has never been greater.

Many have traversed the landscape of dark times alone, or with very little support from those they love. They've traveled far through emotional wildernesses, psychological wastelands, and spiritual deserts. Perhaps they've seen multiple doctors, been to multiple therapists, or experienced their fair share of emergency room visits. Maybe they've tried three or four (or twelve) different medications, various diets, a plethora of exercise programs, or interventions . . . but nothing seems to work. Nothing seems to provide the peace and acceptance their weary souls desire.

This is where He comes in. No, not another doctor, therapist, pet, regimen, or friend (though I am an advocate for all five of those). Someone who understands you better than you understand yourself. Someone who has walked in your shoes yet experienced your pain a thousand-fold. Someone who wept, was betrayed, beaten, mocked, scourged, and crucified.

He is known by many titles, ranging from the Prince of Peace to Savior and Redeemer, to Everlasting Father. But the one that I'd like you to get to know Him by may not be as familiar to you. You may have heard it mentioned in the song "For Unto Us a Child is Born," penned by the great George Frederic Handel . . . the title is *Wonderful Counselor*.

Wonderful is defined as, "Inspiring delight, pleasure, or admiration; extremely good; marvelous."[1]

Counselor is defined as, "A person trained to give guidance on personal, social, or psychological problems."[2]

So quite literally, we have someone available to us who is marvelous, extremely good, and well-trained to give guidance and direction on problems we face in our lives.

The purpose of this book is not to make you believe that a spiritual connection alone can rectify all of your dark times (again, having a holistic approach to healing and thriving is crucial), but rather to introduce a God into your life who understands you and the difficulties you face on a daily basis, and can lend you divine help and assistance as you learn to process them.

Now, I've grown up Christian and have been to church, Sunday school, youth group, and hundreds of other spirit-enhancing activities, but have never been taught a lesson or heard a sermon pertaining to the fact that Jesus Christ is our Wonderful Counselor, willing AND able to help us navigate the soul-crushing times in our individual lives.

So, I decided to write a book about that very fact, with personal examples as well as stories from other great men and women who have journeyed similar roads as me and you. Because if I've learned one thing from living through my own dark times, it is this—knowing that you're not going through it alone and can relate to or find solace in another person's experience can make all the difference in the world. Because that's the thing with journeying through difficult moments—they make us feel isolated. Like nobody understands us. Like we're alone.

Well, you're not alone. I'm here for you. You have Church leaders, friends, family members, doctors, therapists, pets, and other community members who are here for you. And, most importantly, you have an infinitely powerful, all-knowing, all-compassionate, all-loving God who is here for you. His name is Jesus Christ, and from here forward He will be your Wonderful Counselor, a marvelously well-trained guide, offering you strength, comfort, peace, and a listening ear as you put one foot in front of the other on your lifelong journey from darkness to light. So, open the book to whatever chapter best fits your struggle today, and therein find some hope to continue forward.

Chapter 1

Why We All Need a Counselor

For those of you who are friends with me on Facebook, or follow me on Instagram, you are aware that I post personal stories, quotes, and pictures that are vulnerable. I do this because I believe there is a lot of "fluff" out there on social media with people only sharing flawless content, whether that be an ideal vacation to southern Italy, a sculpted body at the gym, or the fifth perfect keto dinner they've made for themselves and their six kids this week. Though definitely fun, and no doubt well-deserved, for the vast majority of us who are simply trying to survive the day-to-day grind of life, these posts can leave us with a feeling of, "Gosh, I wish my life were like that. I don't go to the gym, have enough money to take vacations, or feed my kids perfect dinners (if we even gather around the table for dinner at all). I'll never be good enough."

Amongst pictures of my family, or announcements of a new book I'm working on or have just come out with, I make it a goal to post content that people can relate with on a personal level in the hopes of inspiring those around me and helping them believe that they're not alone as they face their own personal life battles. Because if one thing is a constant in life, that all human beings have in common, it's this—we all struggle, and we are all looking for someone to empathize with our pain.

One day I posted a caption that read, "Today, I'm going to counseling. It's been a rough few weeks, to be honest. Anxiety has been high, I've had a few serious breakdowns/panic attacks, and I may need a change in my medication soon. There's a lot of uncertainty about the future. But you know what? I'm going to counseling! I'm going to talk, to learn, and to heal. Needing counseling isn't a personal failure. Seeing a counselor isn't a sign of weakness. Considering counseling doesn't mean you're crazy. If you're struggling, reach up, reach out, and get the help you *deserve*—for we all deserve to feel heard, loved, and understood."

I received many positive comments from friends and strangers that read,

"Shout it from the rooftops!"

"It's a great reminder we can all do hard things!"

"You're brave. You're enough and you matter."

"Thank you, just thank you."

But, about two hours after I posted, there was a lady who sent me a private message. I noticed that we had been Facebook friends for a few months, so it must have been clear to her where I stood on counseling, mental health, and their legitimacy and fragility having read personal stories of my own life journey involving being bullied, going through anxiety and depression, experiencing suicide ideation, and the like. She said,

> *Why do you allow yourself to believe counseling will help you through your darkest times? Shrinks are for crazy people.*

The question both horrified me and made me chuckle at the same time.

I couldn't fathom the possibility of someone in 2022 still having the paradigm of "counseling is for crazy people who simply *think themselves* into soul-tormenting experiences."

WHAT IS COUNSELING?

Counseling, like therapy, allows people to speak out what is in their mind without having a feeling of being judged or commented on. It also provides a way to self-discovery, self-acceptance, and brings mental peace. Counseling can lead you to a path where you can express what you feel and bring about clarification and validation in your life.

BENEFITS OF COUNSELING

1. Leads to Self-discovery

One of the main advantages of individual counseling is that counseling helps you in self-discovery. Knowing yourself is one of the hardest and most important things to attain to lead a peaceful and successful life.

2. Develop Confidence, Hope, and Encouragement

Another important counseling benefit is the development of confidence, hope, encouragement, and motivation. Motivation and hope will give you the strength to encounter problems in life and take a step further in achieving the goal. Confidence will make your character strong and charms your personality.

3. Helps in The Management of Emotions

Expressing emotions and feelings can be very difficult to handle and manage. There are times when you may have confused feelings. Talking to a counselor can help you in managing your emotions.

4. Contribute to Self-acceptance

You may encounter situations when you may feel worthless and undeserving. This is where counseling will help you in realizing your worth and help you take steps toward self-acceptance.

5. Give Your Point of View a Direction

Another advantage of individual counseling is that it will give your point of view a direction. It presents before you the different aspects of a situation, analyze it, and think of it accurately.

6. Provides Mental Peace

Mental peace is something that everyone wishes to claim these days. We think of making our lives peaceful, but it can't truly be a life of peace until you have mental peace. Counseling can help clear out unnecessary stuff from your mind and help you to relax.

7. Improve Your Skill

Counseling can also help you with improving your abilities. Skills like decision-making, communication, time management, and problem-solving are all needed at various times throughout life, and who better to help you master those than a counselor.

8. Helps in Improving Lifestyle

With advancements in everything from technology to food to education, our lifestyle has also changed a lot. With lifestyle change, a lot of other changes are brought as well. Consulting a counselor gives you the power to resolve positively many changes in your life.

9. Give Insight to Problems

Another benefit of counseling is that it provides you with insight into problems. It helps you understand others' points and think over them. Many times, we are unable to think of both aspects of problems and thus unable to tackle them. A counselor helps you see the other side of problems and helps you handle them.

10. Contributing to Overcoming Addictions

Addiction to drugs, alcohol, or pornography is very harmful, and coming over from it is also not easy at all. Counseling can aid you in turning from negative habits and addictions towards more effective solutions to life's challenges.

11. Eradicate Negative Emotions

Another benefit of counseling is that it wipes out all the negativity within you and gives you the strength to fight the problem. It helps you have a positive approach to life and see things from a very different perspective.[3]

Remember, dark times in life are no respecter of persons. Simply put, anyone can find themselves struggling with them at any point in their lives—regardless of how they've behaved in the past. An event, experience, circumstance, or relationship can cause such trauma to the brain that it changes an individual's future forever.

They can happen to any of us at any time. So please, let's be kind. Let's lend a listening ear. Let's treat everyone with love and respect. Let's get rid of the biases and stigmas surrounding counseling, therapy, or any circumstance that would place an individual therein. Seeking out a counselor or going to counseling does not equate to being weak in any facet; in fact, I would argue that those who exude the most strength, willingly accept their need for a little extra help.

Now that we've covered the *why* behind needing a counselor, we are going to get into the nitty-gritty of *how* our Wonderful Counselor will help us individually and specifically to cope with and eventually overcome each and every one of our dark days, whether they last weeks, months, or years. We are going to do that by taking an in-depth look into scriptures, stories, and experiences shared by those who dealt with these difficult moments personally. Let's get started!

Chapter 2

Jesus Counsels Those with Anxiety about the Future

Anxiety is tough, not only to live with but to describe, as everyone deals with it differently. For me, the strongest way it manifests itself is through irrational fear and worry about the future. Notice how I said *irrational*. Meaning, I know what I'm anxious about may not even be true . . . No, actually probably isn't true at all, but my mind *believes* it's true. Whether that's a decision that needs to be made tomorrow or an event that is coming up in eight months, the symptoms of fear manifest the same: tightness in my chest, heart racing, insomnia, indecision, dry mouth, worry-filled thoughts, tremors, irritation, and the like. It's a killer, and it's something that I consistently work on day by day to live with. Perhaps you do too.

This is where our Counselor comes in.

Whether in a Sunday school, bible study, or personal reading, you may have had the opportunity to come across the scripture in Matthew 6:34 (KJV) which simply states:

> *Take therefore no thought for the morrow: for the morrow shall take thought for the things of itself. Sufficient unto the day is the evil thereof.*

Since those 26 words were spoken over 2,000 years ago, many individuals have rejected them on the basis of confusion. They have rejected those words as a counsel of perfection, as a bit of mysticism.

"I must take thought for the morrow," they say.

"I must take out insurance to protect my family."

"I must prepare a rainy-day fund."

"I must plan carefully for the future so I can get ahead!"

Of course, you must! The truth is those words spoken by Jesus as part of the Sermon on the Mount, translated over 2,000 years ago, don't mean today what they meant during the reign of King James. Long ago the word *thought* frequently meant *anxiety* or *worry*. Modern versions of the bible quote Jesus more accurately for our time as saying, "Therefore do not worry about tomorrow, for tomorrow will worry about itself. Each day has enough trouble of its own" (NIV).

By all means, take thought for tomorrow. Yes, careful thought and planning, but try not to *worry* about tomorrow. (I know, I know, easier said than done.)

Here are some more lessons we can learn from Jesus's teaching here:

In a quote attributed to Mark Twain: "*Worrying is like paying a debt you don't owe.*"[4]

A Christian life should be characterized by our righteous actions, not by an attitude of worry or fretting about what may happen tomorrow.

Worry is a misuse of valuable time.

Another quote attributed to Mark Twain says, "*I've lived through some terrible things in my life, some of which actually happened.*"[5]

Typically, when we worry about tomorrow, next week, or next month, we are imagining the worst possible scenario. We are anxiously anticipating what *may* happen, based not on fact, but on our own perceptions of what could be . . . and that, my friends, is not a good use of our time.

HOW TO STOP WORRYING

We don't worry because we enjoy it. We worry because we are unable (or unwilling) to control it. But worry, as with any emotion, can be trained. Here are four ways to stop worrying:

1. Identify the object of your worry.

Don't fret over consequences, risks, or potential catastrophes, but focus on the object of the worry—what exactly is causing you to worry. Once you've done that, write it down. If there's more than one object of your worry, or more than one worry itself, make a list. Then, turn your worry list into a prayer list. Pray about each one of the things you are worrying about. As Philippians 4:6 (NLT) so brilliantly advises, "Don't worry about anything; instead, pray about everything. Tell God what you need and thank him for all he has done."

2. Either you control the worry, or the worry controls you.

Set aside a 5–10-minute period each day for thinking about problems. This allows you to compartmentalize your worries and not have them rummage through your day. If you find yourself thinking about the problems outside that window, stop and prompt yourself to think about something else (i.e. replace the worry with a different thought) or *do* something else (e.g. exercise, read a book, spend time with loved ones) to replace the worry. Mastering your thoughts can be difficult but will become easier with practice.

3. Don't just worry, find solutions as well.

During your "worry time," remember to contemplate all possible solutions to the worry instead of just the worry itself. Relating to the first step, write it down. Is what you're worried about most likely not going to happen? If it does happen, can you accept it? If you accept it, can you start to think of proactive solutions to help you work through it? Remember, as Charles Kettering put it, "A problem well-stated is a problem half solved." In addition, this is a good time to consider whether or not your worry is valid. Are you blowing things out of proportion? Are you being unrealistic? If you're going to worry about things that in all likelihood will never happen, the least you can do is write them down and try to clear your head.

4. Understand that we don't want to suppress all worry.

Those who try to suppress all unwanted thoughts end up being more distressed by those thoughts. Rather, we want to accept the worry and act on it. Taking action allows us to move past the worry in a constructive, rather than a destructive way. Are we going to sit and stew, or are we going to go and do? In the words of Alfred Lord Tennyson, "I must lose myself in action lest I wither in despair."

During the Second World War, our military leaders *planned* for the morrow, but they could not afford to have any anxiety. Admiral Ernest J. King, who directed the United States Navy, said,

> *I have supplied the best men with the best equipment we have and have given them what seems to be the wisest mission. That is all I can do. If a ship has been sunk, I can't bring it up. If it is going to be sunk, I can't stop it. I can use my time much better working on tomorrow's problem than by fretting about yesterday's. Besides, if I let those things get me, I wouldn't last long.*[6]

Another example of following this scripture comes from Arthur Hays Sulzberger, publisher of *The New York Times*, one of the most famous newspapers in the world.

When he experienced a crisis in his own life that traumatized him, he became so worried about the future he found it almost impossible to sleep. He would frequently get out of bed in the middle of the night, take some canvas and tubes of paint, look in the mirror, and try to paint a portrait of himself. He didn't know anything about painting, but he painted anyway to try and get his mind off of his worries.

According to someone who interviewed Mr. Sulzberger, he was never able to banish his worries and find peace until he adopted as his life motto five words from a church hymn: "One step enough for me."

Lead, kindly Light, amid th'encircling gloom,
Lead Thou me on;
The night is dark, and I am far from home,
Lead Thou me on;
Keep Thou my feet; I do not ask to see
The distant scene; one step enough for me.[7]

Regardless of the mental or emotional pain we may be facing in our lives, it can be so difficult to have any hope for the future. Forget about next week or next month—even contemplating one hour from now can sometimes fill us with such angst and fear that we don't want to move from our beds.[8]

I would ask that you think of a life motto you can adopt that may help you utilize the words of Jesus and "take no anxiety for the morrow," or similarly, live one step at a time.

Here are a few examples you could choose from:

- I am more than a conqueror through Him who loves me. (Based on Romans 8:37)
- God will provide what I cannot see. (Based on Luke 12:22–34).
- I can do all things through Christ. (Based on Philippians 4:13)
- Nothing is impossible as I rely on Jesus. (Based on Luke 1:37).
- If I can believe it, I can achieve it. (Based on Mark 9:23)

Remember, Jesus loves to help those who are anxious about the future. Jesus loves to help turn worry into worship. If we don't know the way, we can remember He *is* the way. If we don't know the truth, we can remember He *is* the truth. He will help us overcome our worry and anxiety about the future and turn our thoughts towards making the present moment the best and most fulfilling it can be as we seek Him and His wisdom.

Chapter 3

Jesus Counsels Those Who
Are Overwhelmed

One of the most comforting scriptures I've ever heard comes from the Old Testament (I say 'heard' because I've actually never read the Old Testament front to back . . . maybe you can relate. If you have read it, you have my greatest admiration). It's great for the individual who is fighting a mental, emotional, or spiritual battle but just can't quite seem to "get over the hump" metaphorically. Perhaps it's a battle stemming from a chronic illness, a wayward child, a form of trauma, or the like. You're tired . . . maybe even exhausted. You can't stop thinking about it, yet at the same time, you wish you could just STOP thinking about it for five minutes because you're so overwhelmed.

It's easy to get overwhelmed in our world, and I think I know why . . . because there's too much of everything.

There's too much news.

There's too much information.

There are too many emails.

There's too much social media.

Heck, there are too many kinds of toothpaste in the grocery store.

A lot of people are overwhelmed by debt. "I'm just never going to get these loans paid off," they cry.

A lot of people are overwhelmed by work. "I can't keep up. There's too much work to do and I never get a break," they lament.

A lot of people are overwhelmed with emotions such as guilt, shame, regret, worry, anger, grief, loneliness, or insecurity.

What's the first thing you do when you feel overwhelmed? Check social media? Play video games? Eat some ice cream? Indulge in your favorite show on Netflix or Hulu?

My go-to is ice cream—Brownie Batter Core Ben and Jerry's. Can't be beaten.

But, in the spirit of this chapter, may I make a suggestion that will give greater peace and clarity in the long run?

Turn to God for help. Why? Keep reading. We'll get there.

To be fair, some people may not turn to ice cream or social media or Netflix. They may get productive and start to plan when they first become overwhelmed. Now, planning is good, and we ought to plan, but let's pray before we plan. Let's turn to God before we turn to our plan.

To create a life where overwhelming situations don't turn into impossible-to-get-through situations, prayer should be our first choice, not our last resort (Matthew 6:33).

Here's the good news, there's no problem too small for you to pray about, and there's no problem too big for you to pray about. If it's big enough to become overwhelmed by, it's big enough to pray about. If it's small enough to become overwhelmed by, it's small enough to pray about.

Where focus goes, energy flows. When we focus on what is overwhelming us, that thing increases. When we focus on God, the solution to what is overwhelming us becomes clearer.

Corrie Ten Boom eloquently put it this way,

If you look at the world, you'll be distressed. If you [fearfully] look within, you'll be depressed. If you look at Christ, you'll be at rest.

It all depends on what we focus on.

The bigger we realize God is, the smaller our problems seem.

As Rick Warren said,

Problems shrink when God expands in our lives.[9]

Ok, I get it. You feel like I've been preaching to you the last 300 words and you're about to throw up. Well, hold onto it for a little while longer because there's been a purpose to it all. I'm about to get to that scripture I teased you about at the beginning of the chapter. But first, let me tell you how the scripture came to be.

Jehoshaphat was a Judean king. In 2 Chronicles 20, the Moabites, Ammonites, and some of the Meunites came to wage war against him. Understandably, some of the people were terrified. They brought their fears to the king and exclaimed (paraphrasing),

"They're coming to get you! A whole lot of people are coming from beyond the sea, and they're coming for you!"

Jehoshaphat was overwhelmingly afraid and rightly so. The Judean army was nothing in comparison to the greater armies of Moab, Ammon, and Meunim. How would such a tiny nation withstand the attack of their more powerful enemies? I think I know . . . they'd be crushed. But Jehoshaphat did not put his trust in the ferocity, money, or the might of his armies. He put his trust in God.

He dropped everything and went to the Lord. He commanded a fast throughout the land. This was a man who knew that the battle was not his to fight or to win, it belonged to Him whose power is mightier than any earthly force (Matthew 8:27).

In his prayer in 2 Chronicles 20:6–12, he recognized the sovereignty of God. To sum it up he said,

> *"God, you created the heavens and the earth. There's nobody greater than you. A whole lot of people are coming to destroy us. You have the power to stop them. With you on our side, we can prevail against them. So here we are, humbly bowed before you, asking for help, for grace, for mercy. Hear us and come to our aid."*

The entire country stood before the Lord, waiting for an answer. Would God deliver them? Would He fight on their behalf as He had done so many times in the past?

The response was swift:

> *Be not afraid nor dismayed by reason of this great multitude, for the battle is not yours, but God's. To morrow go ye down against them . . . Ye will not need to fight in this battle: set yourselves, stand ye still, and see the salvation of the Lord with you, O Judah and Jerusalem: fear not, nor be dismayed; to morrow go out against them: for the Lord will be with you (2 Chronicles 20:15–17, KJV).*

Notice the phrases that are used in this passage:

Ye will not need to fight.
Set [position] yourself.
Stand ye still, and see.
Fear not.
The Lord will be with you.

There are a lot of action words here, but it's clearly conveyed that, when overwhelmed, all God's people have to do is be obedient and submissive to God and He will do the rest.

I can sense someone reading this with pessimism, thinking to themselves,

"Yes Drew, that's all very easy for you to write . . . but c'mon . . . of course, I need to act. Of course, I need to plan and prepare . . . I can't just 'give it to God' and do nothing."

I agree. 100%. No question. You see, I don't believe that when God asks us to "stand still" it equates to "do absolutely nothing." Rather, I believe that God intends for us to continue with our day-to-day lives. If we work, then it's important that we go to work. If we are in school, then it's important to go to school. If we take care of our family, it's important to continue doing that. We're not being asked to simply "wave the white flag," shut ourselves up in our rooms, and pretend the outside world doesn't exist.

Rather, our faith and trust are manifested in our ability to say,

"God, I am doing all I can right now to try and figure out this situation. I'm tired. I'm ready to give up. I need you to take care of it. I can't fight much longer."

To which God responds,

"Leave it in my hands and trust me. I have a plan for you that you cannot see, but which will be made manifest soon enough."

Question: Has God ever lost a battle?
Answer: No.

God has never lost a battle He has chosen to fight. He's God. He doesn't lose battles, He wins. Now, He may not show up when we expect Him to, and it may be after we've seemingly exhausted all our physical and emotional resources, but without a doubt, He shows up and He fights (and wins) that battle for us.

Remember, you are on the winning side. God loves you just as much as He loved Jehoshaphat, and He will provide for you just as He provided for him. You may not be physically preparing for an entire army to come against you, but you may be a single parent trying to hold it all together. You may be a young married couple trying to finish school, start a family, and survive financially. You may be overwhelmed with depression, anxiety, cancer, discouragement, or exhaustion. You may have just been laid off from work and can't comprehend how you'll make it through. Those are all battles fought in the lonely foxholes of the heart. Jesus is saying the same thing to you today,

"My child, you will not need to fight. Position yourself. Stand still and see my salvation. Do not be afraid. I am with you."

The battle is not yours, give it over to Jesus, allow Him to counsel you, and see the miraculous victory that occurs.

Chapter 4

Jesus Counsels Those Who Have a Hard Time Trusting

The unknown. It can be a scary place to find yourself in. Whether emotionally, physically, mentally, or spiritually, not knowing the outcome of something can bring such fear into your life that the ability to act becomes diminished and your trust becomes squelched.

What do we do when we find ourselves struggling with the unknown?

What do we do when we recognize that we don't have all the answers and that we may not know what the outcome of a certain situation will be?

Do we panic, or do we pray?

Do we worry, or do we worship?

Do we wait in fear, or act in faith?

My favorite scripture pertaining to the topic of trusting God comes from the books of Proverbs in the bible. Proverbs 3:5 (KJV) says,

Trust in the Lord with all thine heart; and lean not unto thine own understanding.

The most important part of that scripture, in my opinion, is where God tells us to not lean unto our own understanding. He knows we are emotional beings. He knows when it comes to making decisions, in terms of eternity and how long He has been God for, we are infants. We allow hunger, fatigue, anger, anxiety, fear, illness, and other ailments to hinder our judgment. We don't always have it figured out. Hence, He gives us counsel only a loving Father would provide . . .

"Son. Daughter. I know you. I know your life. I know what the plan is. I know you think you know what is best, but you don't. Trust me. Lean on me. Rely on me. Cast this over on me. I will not lead you astray."

One of my most admired scripture heroes is Moses. I believe that he is a prime example of what trusting in God is, regardless of the immediate uncertainties you face.

God's people, the Israelites, had been enslaved by the pharaoh in Egypt for many years. Now, through a series of miracles (plagues) performed by Moses through God's power, they were finally free to leave and go make a home in their very own land.

Over 600,000 Israelites set off (Exodus 12:37–38) and followed Moses. He always knew which direction to go because God put an angel and a pillar of cloud in front of them to point the way. At night they followed a pillar of fire. They never got lost because God always showed the correct way to go.

Eventually, the pillar stopped by the water called the Red Sea. The Israelites camped by water and waited for what God wanted them to do next.

Meanwhile, back in Egypt, Pharaoh and his officials began thinking about how all of the Israelites had left. God had proven, through the ten plagues, that He was more powerful than the King of Egypt and all of the Egyptian gods. At that time, Pharaoh and the people had told the Israelites to leave Egypt, but now they were having second thoughts. If all the slaves left Egypt, they thought, then who would do all the work?

So, Pharaoh decided to chase after the Israelites and make them come back. He sent all of his horses and chariots and all of his horsemen and troops. He must have thought,

"NO ONE would be able to stop this army!"

When God's people saw the Egyptian army approaching in the distance, they became very fearful. There was nowhere to go to get away. The army was behind them, and the Red Sea was in front of them. They were trapped!

The people complained to Moses. They cried,

Was it because there were no graves in Egypt that you brought us to the desert to die? What have you done to us by bringing us out of Egypt? Didn't we say to you in Egypt, "Leave us alone; let us serve the Egyptians"? It would have been better for us to serve the Egyptians than to die in the desert!" (Exodus 14:11–12, NIV)

Moses answered them with power that could've only come from God,

Do not be afraid. Stand firm and you will see the deliverance the Lord will bring you today. The Egyptians you see today you will never see again. The Lord will fight for you; you need only to be still. (Exodus 14:13–14, NIV)

Now amazing things began to happen right before their very eyes. The people had thought that they were trapped because of the water, but they were about to see that God is so powerful He can do anything!

The angel of God who had been traveling in front of the Israelites moved back behind them along with the pillar of cloud. The back of the cloud blocked the view of the Egyptians, and they could only see night and darkness. The front of the cloud provided light for God's people so they could see everything.

They could see the Red Sea in front of them and wished they could get across the sea to safety.

Then the Lord said to Moses,

Tell the Israelites to move on. Raise your staff and stretch out your hand over the sea to divide the water so that the Israelites can go through the sea on dry ground. (Exodus 14:16–17, NIV)

Moses did as He was asked.

At that very moment, a strong wind blew the water up into two walls so that there was dry land down the middle for the Israelites to cross through.

When the Egyptians saw the dry land, they followed the Israelites. Do you think they caught up with them? No, they did not. Strange things began happening to them. The wheels of their chariots began falling off and it became very difficult to drive. By the time the Egyptians realized God was fighting against them, it was too late.

Now that the Israelites were all safely on the other side, God told Moses to stretch his staff over the water again. He did so, and just as swiftly and perfectly as the water parted, it came crashing back to its earthly form, drowning all the armies of the Egyptians in the process.

What's your "Red Sea" that you're up against right now?

What's the situation in your life that's causing you so much fear you find it difficult to trust God?

Do you have enemies, metaphorical or literal, chasing after you right now?

Now is the time to trust. Now is the time to *lean into* the unknown and the uncertainty. Now is the time to pledge complete submission and surrender to the will of God, utilizing the words of Jesus as our example,

Not my will, but Thine, be done. (Luke 22:42, KJV)

It'll be hard. It'll seem crazy—both to yourself and to those around you—but it's the right thing to do. And even if it's just one step ahead of you, that's all you need. Remember chapter 2? Lead, Kindly Light.

Author Lynn Austin couldn't have said it any better,

Faith don't come in a bushel basket, Missy. It come one step at a time. Decide to trust Him for one little thing today, and before you know it, you find out He's so trustworthy you be putting your whole life in His hands.[10]

Remember, there is no greater joy than seeing God's destiny for us rise above our current circumstances. He is an "outside-the-box" thinker. He sees things we cannot. He hears conversations we cannot. He knows the hearts of individuals we do not. And above all, He loves us more than we can comprehend (Romans 5:8). Think of someone you know who loves you tremendously. They may be a parent, spouse, partner, sibling, aunt, uncle, cousin, or friend. Now take that love and multiply it by infinity, and that equates to God's love for you. Would you not feel secure in trusting that love?

The Israelites felt backed up against a wall with no way out, but that's because no one would have predicted that God would part the Red Sea for them to walk through on the solid ground.

Difficult times will happen to us all. Though it is easy to get afraid of having nowhere to turn, these are the moments we can see God work at His best as we trust Him and move forward one step at a time.

Chapter 5

Jesus Counsels Those Who Are Discouraged

Discouragement. It's an affliction that seems to reach every individual throughout the course of their lives. Doesn't matter what socioeconomic status you experience, what color your skin is, what gender you identify as, what background you come from, or what clothes you wear—it will always come and find you.

The key is not in never going throughout life being discouraged (which is impossible), but in knowing where to turn when you experience it for yourself.

1 Peter 5:7 (KJV) beautifully reads,

Casting all your care upon him; for he careth for you.

Ah, that's nice. Reading that verse is like taking a drink of ice-cold water on a hot summer's day. It's refreshing, rejuvenating, and recharging.

Humans often overestimate their ability and underestimate their inability. Yet the humble recognize that they are not God. God is all-powerful, all-knowing, and able to handle all our cares. As a humble person, you can cast all your care on Him because you know He cares for you. To "cast" literally means to "throw." It is from the same Greek word used to describe how the people threw their coats on the colt before Jesus rode it into Jerusalem on Palm Sunday (Luke 19:35). We should not hold onto our cares. Instead, we should throw them to our Wonderful Counselor who cares for us. He has big shoulders; He can handle our burdens.

Cares refer to worries, difficulties and needs of this world, and anxieties. The NLT says to "give all your worries and cares to God," and the NIV says to "cast all your anxiety on him." Everything that worries us or weighs us down is to be given to the God who cares so deeply for us. These verses do not promise that God will fix or remove our concerns. Instead, the assurance is in knowing that He cares for us, which is why we can cast our cares on Him. God is trustworthy and we can trust Him to handle our cares in the best way. Romans 8:28 tells us that God works all things for the good of those who love Him and are called according to His purpose. We trust that God is able and willing to deal with our cares.

Jesus also invited people to cast their cares on Him:

Come to me, all you who are weary and burdened, and I will give you rest. Take my yoke upon you and learn from me, for I am gentle and humble in heart, and you will find rest for your souls. For my yoke is easy and my burden is light. (Matthew 11:28–30, NIV)

Jesus calls us to come to Him and cast our cares or burdens on Him. When we do, the promise is that we will find rest for our souls. The assurance is based on who He is. We can come to Him with any of our concerns in prayer, and, while the burden may still exist, our souls will find rest as we trust in Him to help us carry it and to sustain us through the trial.

Peter's exhortation to humble ourselves and to cast all our cares on the Lord is a command, not a suggestion. We are commanded to trust in the Lord and not in ourselves (Proverbs 3:5) and to be anxious for nothing (Philippians 4:6). God does not want us to be weighed down by the discouraging moments and worries of this life. Instead, He cares for us and promises rest for all who come to Him.

Discouragement happens for a variety of reasons. Maybe that's why it's addressed so frequently in scripture.

- Job was discouraged because of his family and friends (Book of Job).
- Elijah became discouraged after a huge victory (1 Kings 19).
- Jeremiah was discouraged with God (Lamentations 3).
- Jesus's disciples were discouraged after His death (Luke 24:20–21).
- Peter was discouraged with himself (Matthew 26).

The insight gained from these individuals along with other scripture gives us valuable instruction for dealing with our own discouragement. I'd like to recommend six steps we can take today to help.

HONESTLY ACKNOWLEDGE FEELINGS

This happens with all of the individuals listed above. Being honest with yourself is crucial for opening your mind and spirit to encouragement and hope. In fact, it may just be the first requirement for transitioning from being discouraged to being encouraged.

TAKE CARE OF YOURSELF PHYSICALLY

God sets the example for this with Elijah. Before addressing Elijah's discouragement, God makes sure Elijah is nourished, hydrated, and rested. We simply cannot overcome discouragement without taking care of ourselves physically and mentally too.

THINK ABOUT WHAT YOU'RE THINKING ABOUT

Both Jeremiah and Elijah do this, and we are encouraged to do so as well, both through their examples and through other scripture that addresses our thought lives.

> *Finally, brothers and sisters, whatever is true, whatever is noble, whatever is right, whatever is pure, whatever is lovely, whatever is admirable—if anything is excellent or praiseworthy—think about such things. (Philippians 4:8, NIV)*

> *We demolish arguments and every pretension that sets itself up against the knowledge of God, and we take captive every thought to make it obedient to Christ. (2 Corinthians 10:5, NIV)*

RETRAIN YOUR BRAIN

This is especially important if discouragement has become like a shadow. Retraining your brain essentially involves cleaning out unhelpful thought patterns and replacing them with ones that promote growth and open you up to encouragement.

A mindset that is able to ward off continued discouragement is one that acknowledges and accepts that life is hard and that focuses on knowing that God will create value and purpose out of what you're going through.

> *We are hard pressed on every side, but not crushed; perplexed, but not in despair; persecuted, but not abandoned; struck down, but not destroyed. We always carry around in our body the death of Jesus, so*

that the life of Jesus may also be revealed in our body. For we who are alive are always being given over to death for Jesus' sake, so that his life may also be revealed in our mortal body. So then, death is at work in us, but life is at work in you. (2 Corinthians 4:8–12, NIV)

Now I want you to know, brothers and sisters, that what has happened to me has actually served to advance the gospel. As a result, it has become clear throughout the whole palace guard and to everyone else that I am in chains for Christ. And because of my chains, most of the brothers and sisters have become confident in the Lord and dare all the more to proclaim the gospel without fear. (Philippians 1:12–14, NIV).

PRESS IN CLOSE TO GOD

Life is hard. People disappoint. And God's ways aren't always clear or make sense. Pressing close to God acknowledges your trust in Him regardless of circumstances.

The Lord is good, a refuge in times of trouble. He cares for those who trust in him. (Nahum 1:7, NIV)

CHASE OUT NEGATIVE FEELINGS

Getting rid of negativity is important, but it only works long term if we replace it with thankfulness.

Give thanks in all circumstances; for this is God's will for you in Christ Jesus. (1 Thessalonians 5:18, NIV)

When I get discouraged, I revisit the stories in the scriptures of others who also experienced discouragement, as well as the many verses that speak to how to defeat a mindset of discouragement. Doing so reminds me of God's activity as well as gives me specific ways to move away from a mindset of negativity and discouragement and toward one of hope and peace in Him.

Remember, we all have occasion to feel the discouragement that is so prevalent in today's world. Those who cast their cares on the Lord, take care of themselves mentally and emotionally, follow the examples of those gone before them who have traversed similar paths, and never give up will taste the sweet fruit of overcoming. It may not be next week or next month, but it will come at a time when the lesson we needed to learn is ingrained within our souls like a tattoo on our hearts—serving as a constant reminder of where we've been, in whom we have trusted, and our ability to face similar circumstances knowing we can make it through!

Chapter 6

Jesus Counsels Those Who Have a Hard Time Letting Go of Control

Surrender. It's not a word that many people grow up wanting to make efficacious in their lives. In a culture where we live by such maxims as "grit your teeth and bear it," "last one standing wins," "suck it up," and "play through the pain," many find the word 'surrender' synonymous with defeat, loss, giving up, or retreat.

That, however, is false. With God, letting go and surrendering is a beautiful sign of maturing—a maturity that comes from confidence and humility in who He is and His plan for our lives, not in who we are and the plan we have for ourselves.

In our Wonderful Counselor's own words,

O my Father, if it be possible, let this cup pass from me: nevertheless not as I will, but as thou wilt. (Matthew 26:39, KJV)

Jesus could've fought it or tried to control the situation more fully. He could've called down legions of angels to protect Him. He could've turned any of the Roman guards into a pillar of salt with the blink of an eye. But He didn't. Christ surrendered. Not only to those who scourged and defiled Him but to His father who knew that only by completing the Atonement and Resurrection could immense redemption follow.

I've noticed that things go much more smoothly when I give up control—when I *allow* them to happen instead of *making* them happen. Unfortunately, I'm terrible at this. To sum it up the best way I know how, as long as everything is going the exact way I want it too, I'm totally flexible. Can I get an amen?

Although I'm much better than I used to be, I'm a bit of a control freak. I often use perfectly good energy trying to plan, predict, and prevent things that I cannot possibly plan, predict, or prevent.

For example, I wonder if my toddler is going to get a proper nap when we travel and, if not, just how crabby she might be. I think through her travel and napping patterns, attempting to figure out exactly what we're up against as if her sleep is something I can control.

Like most humans I know, I spend a lot of time in business that's not mine. The baby's business, my wife's business, God's business.

As a recovering control freak, there are three things I know for sure about trying to control things:

1. We try to control things because of what we think will happen if we don't.

In other words, control is rooted in fear.

2. Control is a result of being attached to a specific outcome—an outcome we're sure is best for us, as if we always know what's best.

There is power in the verse from Isaiah 55:8 (NIV),

> *For my thoughts are not your thoughts, neither are your ways my ways, declares the Lord.*

When we trust that we're okay no matter what circumstances come our way, we don't need to micromanage the universe. We let go. And we open ourselves to all sorts of wonderful possibilities that aren't there when we're attached to one "right" path.

3. The energy of surrender accomplishes much more than the energy of control.

I suspect it's slightly different for everyone, but here's what control mode looks and feels like for me: My vision gets very narrow and focused, my breath is shallow, adrenaline is pumping, and my heart rate increases. My mind shifts from topic to topic and from past to future very quickly, and I have little concentration, poor memory, and almost no present-moment awareness. In surrender mode, I'm calm, and peaceful. Breathing deeply, present in the moment. I see clearly and my vision extends out around me, allowing me to (literally) see the bigger picture. So, the great irony is that attempting to control things actually feels *less* in control. When I'm micromanaging and obsessing over details, I know I'm in my own way—even if I temporarily get what I want.

THE ART OF SURRENDER

Surrender literally means to stop fighting. Stop fighting with yourself. Stop fighting God's plan and the natural flow of things. Stop resisting and pushing against reality.

Surrender = Complete acceptance of what is + faith that all is well, even without my input.

It's not about inaction. It's about acting from that place of surrender energy.

If letting go of control and surrendering not only feels better but actually produces better results, then how do we do that? Sometimes it's as easy as noticing that you're in control mode and choosing to let go—consciously and deliberately shifting into surrender and trust energy.

For example, when I become aware that I'm in control mode, I imagine that I'm in a small boat paddling upstream, against the current. It's hard. It's a fight. That's what control mode feels like to me. When I choose to let go, surrender, and trust God to provide what I cannot see, I visualize the boat turning around, me dropping the oars, and floating downstream. I'm being gently pulled, no strenuous effort necessary on my part. Simply breathing and saying, "Let go of the oars," is usually enough to get me there.

That being said, sometimes it's a little harder to make the shift from control to surrender. Here are a few questions that may help:

1. What am I afraid will happen if I let go of control?

When you pinpoint the fear, question its validity. Ask yourself, Is it true? If you're afraid the night will be ruined if your boyfriend doesn't remember to pick up eggplant (and you've already reminded him fourteen times), question that assumption. Can you really know the night would be *ruined* without the eggplant? And if it would be ruined (by your definition, anyway), what's so bad about that? Will you survive? Will it matter in 5 minutes, 5 days, or 5 weeks from now?

2. Find out whose business you're in.

Your business is the realm of things that you can directly influence. Are you there? Or are you in someone else's business? When we're trying to control things outside of our own business, it's not going to go well, and we'll be constantly frustrated because believe it or not—we have very little control over anyone except ourselves.

3. Consider this: Would letting go feel like freedom?

It almost always would. Let that feeling of freedom guide you toward loosening your grip.

A FRIENDLY UNIVERSE

Albert Einstein said, "The most important decision we make is whether we believe we live in a friendly or hostile universe."

I believe in a friendly universe. I believe in a God who genuinely cares for each of us and wants us to be happy and whole.

Being receptive and allowing things to happen is a skill that can be practiced and improved upon. It helps to believe in a friendly God—one who is supporting you at every turn so that you don't have to worry yourself over the details. We can always choose to do things the easy way or the hard way. We can muscle through, or we can let go of the oars and let the current carry us downstream. There is a peaceful, yet focused energy that accompanies holding the intention of what I want, but not forcing myself to do it. That energy is magic. I'm still a work in progress, but I'm *allowing* it to become a habit instead of *making* it a habit.

In her book *Invitation to Silence and Solitude* (2006), Ruth Haley Barton offers this incredible insight, that when we come "face to face with our addiction to control, there is also an invitation: the invitation to let go and allow God to be in control."[11]

Of course, the hardest part about that for so many of us is the reality that when we let go of control, then we can't control the outcome. And if we're honest, we always want to have our hand in controlling outcomes. But there is also incredible freedom to be found here.

If we are brave enough to truly let go of control, to trust God with the outcome, then we exemplify living in faith. So often what we fail to realize is that whenever we try to control outcomes, we are doing the inverse of Proverbs 3:5 . . . instead of "leaning not unto our own understanding" we are only leaning unto our own understanding. When we lay down our desire for control at the feet of Jesus and decide instead to live and walk in faith, believing that God is working all things together for our good and for His ultimate glory, something incredible happens.

Chapter 7

Jesus Counsels Those Who Are Lonely

One of my favorite titles for Jesus is Emmanuel. I think it has such a beautiful meaning: *God with us.* In a world where we may feel left out or left alone because of our mental or emotional handicaps, we have a Savior who comes to our aid.

Loneliness is one of the most crushing human emotions. The feelings of abandonment and isolation create an overwhelming sense of helplessness and despair. People in the throes of a heightened state of loneliness often fall prey to temptations or behaviors that are extremely atypical. It is a dangerous place to be. Jesus knows what it is like to be lonely. As the perfect Son of God, He certainly was unlike all the other children in Nazareth. And we all know that when a person is different from the crowd, they usually spend time by themselves.

Shortly after He began His public ministry, many of the disciples left Him when His teachings became too difficult to grasp. At the time of His greatest sorrow, the handful that remained scattered, leaving Him utterly alone.

As our sympathetic High Priest who "had to be made like His brothers in every way" (Hebrews 2:17, BSB) and who "shared in [our] humanity" (Hebrews 2:14, NIV), Jesus is intimately acquainted with the devastating effect of loneliness.

He is also able to come to our aid with help and hope that can lift us out of the deepest pit.

Jesus hears our hearts cry.

The faintest whisper of a heart that feels alone and abandoned comes before the heart of a loving Lord who will go to any lengths to comfort His children. In fact, He has already gone to the extreme in offering Himself on the cross, and in the Garden of Gethsemane. So, will He not freely give us the help we need in our personal suffering (Romans 8:32)?

A certain story comes to mind to illustrate this point in greater detail. The Bible describes the famous account of Jesus Christ healing a bleeding woman miraculously in three different Gospel reports: Matthew 9:20–22, Mark 5:24–34, and Luke 8:42–48. The woman, who had suffered from a bleeding disorder for twelve years causing her extreme shame, sadness, and loneliness, finally found relief when she reached out to Jesus in a crowd.

While Jesus was walking toward a synagogue leader's house to help his dying daughter, a large crowd followed Him. One of the people in that crowd was a woman who struggled with an illness that caused her to constantly bleed. She had pursued healing for years, but no doctor was able to help her. Then, a miracle happened.

Mark 5:24–29 (NIV) begins the story this way:

A large crowd followed and pressed around him. And a woman was there who had been subject to bleeding for twelve years. She had suffered a great deal under the care of many doctors and had spent all she had, yet instead of getting better, she grew worse.

When she heard about Jesus, she came up behind him in the crowd and touched his cloak, because she thought, "If I just touch his clothes, I will be healed."

Immediately her bleeding stopped, and she felt in her body that she was freed from her suffering.

An overwhelming number of people were in the crowd that day, but the woman was determined to reach Jesus however she could. By this point, Jesus had developed a widespread reputation as a remarkable teacher and healer. Though the woman had sought help from many doctors (and spent all her money in the process as we just read) to no avail, she still had faith that she could finally find healing if she reached out to Jesus.

Not only did the woman have to overcome discouragement in order to reach out, but she also had to overcome shame. The Jewish religion considered women to be ceremonially unclean while they were menstruating. As someone who was considered to be unclean, the woman couldn't worship in the synagogue or enjoy normal social relationships (anyone who touched her while she was bleeding was also considered unclean). Wouldn't this make you feel lonely, and like a societal outcast?

Due to this deep sense of shame, the woman would likely have been afraid to touch Jesus within His sight, so she decided to approach Him as unobtrusively as possible.

Luke describes Jesus's response this way in Luke 8:45–48 (NIV):

"Who touched me?" Jesus asked. When they all denied it, Peter said, "Master, the people are crowding and pressing against you."

But Jesus said, "Someone touched me; I know that power has gone out from me."

Then the woman, seeing that she could not go unnoticed, came trembling and fell at his feet. In the presence of all the people, she told why she had touched him and how she had been instantly healed.

Then he said to her, "Daughter, your faith has healed you. Go in peace."

We see from this story that Christ has immense empathy and love for those of us who for whatever reason, whether it be mental, emotional, physical, or psychological, feel alone . . . like we don't belong . . . like we are outsiders. But, just like the woman with the bleeding disorder, we can take comfort in knowing as soon as we reach out and reach up to Him, we can feel peace, healing, and wholeness.

Throughout the scriptures, when men and women of faith faced great physical, mental, and emotional challenges, God reminded them of His powerful presence, saying to them, "I am with you" (Isaiah 43:5, NIV). They were afraid, anxious, doubtful, and bewildered, but the awareness of God's presence became their strength to deal with formidable odds. Lonely individuals were instilled with courage, lonely prophets with boldness, and lonely apostles with hope.

Remember, *God* is with us. The God who is able. The God who is kind. The God who is gentle. The God who knows all our needs. The God who is faithful. The God who works all things together for *our* good. The God who loves us with an everlasting love.

God has already turned to you through the presence of His Spirit. His face shines upon you. Turn to Him and find the solace and help you need. It may come through a scripture promise. It may come through prayer. It may come through His still voice when you are quiet on your bed or driving home from a long day. Regardless, He is aware, and He will come to help.

Here are nine verses you can turn to whenever you feel lonely:

- **Deuteronomy 31:6**—God is with you in the midst of any and every fearful and difficult circumstance.
- **Psalm 118:6–7**—The Lord is with you! He is your Helper and Victor.
- **Psalm 9:9–10**—The Lord's sheltering presence is safe and reliable. He will never forsake those who seek Him.
- **Psalm 68:5–6**—God draws close to those who are lonely and provides for them. He is a "father to the fatherless" and He "sets the lonely in families."
- **Isaiah 41:10**—God holds you in His hand. He will help you and give you strength.
- **Lamentations 3:22–24**—The Lord is all you need. He is faithful, loving, and compassionate to those who wait for Him.
- **John 14:16–21**—The Lord's presence is permanent and intimate.
- **Romans 8:39**—Nothing can ever separate you from Jesus and His love.
- **2 Timothy 4:16–18**—Even if everyone else deserts you, the Lord will stand at your side and strengthen you.

Even if you *feel* alone, you can trust that God is with you. Ask Him to comfort you with His faithful presence today.

Chapter 8

Jesus Counsels Those Who
Have a Hard Time Forgiving

We've all been there. The in-law who gave you the cold shoulder the first time you met them, the bully in 6th grade who made fun of your weight or the fact that you wore big glasses or baggy t-shirts, the boyfriend or girlfriend who said that one thing while you were dating that rubbed you the wrong way (and still does years later) . . . It's hard to let those things go. We play those scenes over and over again in our minds, blowing them up, and retelling the stories at family dinners or social gatherings so that they're not forgotten.

Why do we have such a hard time forgiving?

Is it because we believe intrinsically that forgiving is synonymous with condoning?

Do we think that by letting go of past hurts we are in some way excusing the behavior that took place and not allowing "justice" to take place?

Maybe. I think it depends on the individual who was hurt, and their relationship with forgiveness. Typically, if we grew up in an environment where forgiveness wasn't practiced, shown, or emphasized, then we don't have a healthy relationship with it, and automatically believe that by holding onto the pain and the hurt, we are somehow holding the perpetrator accountable and making them suffer.

Unfortunately, that's not reality.

In a quote attributed to the Buddha, "Holding onto anger is liking drinking poison and expecting the other person to die."

Thomas S. Monson once said, "Blame keeps wounds open. Only forgiveness heals" ("Love—the Essence of the Gospel," *Ensign*, Apr. 2014, 93).

Now, I'm in no way attempting to minimize anyone's pain who is reading this right now. Pain is pain. Period. There is no reason to try and explain it or defend your pain to anyone else. Whether your trauma came at the hands of bullies, abusers, name-callers, or attackers, you have every right to feel the way you do.

And, it's time to forgive, not because the bullies don't deserve justice—but because you deserve peace. You, my friend, have been locked in a prison for many days now . . . a prison of pain, suffering, agony, and torment (maybe even hate or trauma) . . . and it's time to set yourself free—for you have been the one holding the key to your release this whole time.

One of the beautiful things about Jesus is that He is not merely a great teacher, but the ultimate Teacher: God's message in the flesh. Jesus, therefore, does not simply utter commandments or provide abstract concepts. His very life provides examples of God's Word in action (John 1:1, 14, 18)!

One such command is seen in the book of Luke:

But I say unto you that hear, love your enemies, do good to them that hate you, bless them that curse you, pray for them that despitefully use you. And unto him that smiteth thee on the one cheek offer also the other; and from him that taketh away thy cloak withhold not thy coat also. (Luke 6:27–29, KJV)

Love an enemy? Bless those who curse you? Pray for those who hurt you? These are very difficult things indeed.

Jesus never denies that they are difficult. Instead, He shows you the way by demonstrating the command in Himself, in a circumstance you are rather unlikely to experience!

In the midst of His great suffering on the cross, He petitions His Father to do this very thing: forgive those who are despitefully using Him. As He suffers such great and terrible anguish—anguish that most of us can barely imagine—He still represents God's Word. He still holds firm to God's intentions for the Kingdom.

If Jesus is able to forgive those who nailed His body to the cross, can we not forgive those who may strike us?

If Jesus is able to forgive those who mock Him, can we not forgive those who insult us?

If Jesus is able to forgive those who conspired to have Him killed, can we not forgive those who do not particularly like us or attempt to do evil toward us?

It is not easy. It is rather counter-intuitive. But it was just as counter-intuitive for Jesus. The whole experience of suffering for our sins was likely counterintuitive, yet He accomplished it because He was obedient to God's will and received His power to overcome (Hebrews 5:7–9).

A story about a woman named Victoria exemplifies the principle of forgiveness better than any story I've ever heard in my life.

On a cold winter night in November 2004 six teenagers in Ronkonkoma, New York bought a 20-pound frozen turkey with a stolen credit card. Their plan? To "prank someone" by throwing it out of their car on the highway into oncoming traffic. While driving on Sunrise Highway, 18-year-old Ryan Cushing chucked the turkey out of the back window. The turkey slammed into Victoria Ruvolo's car, shattering her windshield (and her face), nearly killing her in the process. She was taken to the hospital with life-threatening injuries. It wasn't until several weeks later that she awoke from the coma her injuries had put her in, not remembering a single thing about what happened.

In her own words,

When I looked in the mirror, I could see it was me but my whole face was smashed in and every single bone in my face was broken. I had no idea I'd had ten hours of surgery and I was shocked when the doctors told me that from now on, for the rest of my life, I would always have three titanium plates in my left cheek, one in my right cheek, and I'd also have a wire mesh holding my left eye in place because my left eye socket was so badly shattered.

Let's pause the story right here for a moment. Now, you may be thinking to yourself, "That Ryan Cushing is a devil. How could anyone, regardless of their age, not have the common sense, let alone the moral restraint of doing something that horrific. He, no doubt, should receive a life sentence in prison."

That's probably how most of us would react to the downright cruelty of what took place that winter night. But that's not how Victoria reacted, and her story left a lasting impression on millions of others who found themselves in places where forgiveness was an option, but not required.

Months after the accident, and many surgeries, Victoria learned that Cushing was facing a possible 25-year prison sentence for his crime, and that his friends were going to testify against him as part of a plea deal to let them off easy.

She immediately started pestering the prosecution for more information about Cushing.

How was he raised? Why would he do this thing? Was it peer pressure that influenced him? Are there any underlying mental health issues that he's been struggling with?

Now, you may be thinking, "*Who cares* about his 'home life' or 'mental health?' What he did was inexcusable, and most certainly unforgivable."

Again, thank goodness for people like Victoria who live a higher, better way.

After gathering all the information about Cushing that she could, she made a decision that not only changed his life, but the lives of millions of others she had never met—she forgave.

Victoria insisted on a plea deal for Cushing—six months in the county jail and five years' probation—in exchange for pleading guilty.

In a courtroom scene that left every onlooker in tears, she embraced Cushing, telling him with physical handicaps that would never be healed, "I just want you to make your life the best it can be."

Cushing wept in her arms as he apologized profusely for what he had done.

How many of us, when having experienced pain inflicted upon us, or seen it done to a loved one, immediately seek retaliation? Whether we choose to physically get revenge, or rather purposefully go behind the perpetrator's back with gossip or judgment, what is our intent? Is it to seek an eye for an eye? Is it to "teach them a lesson" for messing with us?

Victoria Ruvolo had every right to testify against Cushing. She had everyone *expecting* her to let the judge rule with their 25-year sentence. She had no obligation to forgive and move on—but she did.

> *Some people couldn't understand why I'd done this, but I felt God had given me a second chance and I wanted to pass it on. I know I did the right thing. Kids like Ryan don't think about what they do. They think they're invincible and everything will be OK. They don't think about how every action has a reaction.*

Victoria passed away unexpectedly at the age of 59 in 2019, but her legacy will forever live on through Cushing, those in the courtroom, and everyone who has ever read or heard of her story.[12]

Forgiveness is HARD.

Forgiveness is TOUGH.

Forgiveness is TRYING.

But it's the only way to set ourselves free from the prison of rumination, hatred, and revenge.

As Ghandi, said, "An eye for an eye makes the whole world blind."

Moving forward, let this quote from Najwa Zebian be your motto towards those who have wronged you (or will wrong you) in your life,

Today I decided to forgive you. Not because you apologized, or because you acknowledged the pain that you caused me, but because my soul deserves peace.

Chapter 9

Jesus Counsels Those Who Are Impatient

Waiting can be hard. You may be seeking an answer to a sincere prayer, one that doesn't seem to go much higher than your head when uttered—even though you may crave an immediate response. You may be struggling with anxiety or depression, having tried half a dozen medications or treatments but to no avail, and you're contemplating whether or not you can continue forward. Or, more routinely, you may be sitting on the couch after a long day, and the Smart TV has yet to connect to the WiFi so you can watch your favorite show on Peacock or Netflix . . . you see the 'connecting circle' on the screen continue to spin . . . and spin . . . and spin. You start biting your nails, considering resetting the entire network in the next 10 seconds if the show hasn't loaded by then. Regardless of the situation, it can be very difficult to wait for what we want.

The word *patient* is defined in five ways.[13]

1: bearing pains or trials calmly or without complaint.

2: manifesting forbearance under provocation or strain.

3: not hasty or impetuous.

4: steadfast despite opposition, difficulty, or adversity.

5: able or willing to bear.

Stop reading for 10 seconds and think about if these definitions describe you. Now, think about if these definitions describe the complete *opposite* of you.

For me at least, and call it being part of Gen Z, growing up with a smartphone, or just living in a world with microwaves and Amazon prime, I struggle when it comes to sacrificing what I want in the moment for what I want *more* in the future.

Isn't that what patience really boils down to? It seems like whenever we feel the need to be patient, it's because we know deep down (even if we don't want to admit it) that if we wait, the thing we are waiting for will be of greater worth than if we just bailed and took the easy way out. Now, I'm not saying that with every case. Sometimes it's important to let things go and choose the option that will "get you where you want to go faster" (i.e. Flying across the country instead of driving if you have an urgent deadline to hit, driving your pregnant wife to the hospital instead of taking the tandem bike when she's in labor, or taking the elevator to the top of the Empire State Building instead of climbing the stairs, etc.). But much of the time, when it comes to decisions of importance and significance, the greater ability we have to be patient—to wait—will translate into a greater manifestation of fulfillment and happiness in our lives.

There have been many times throughout history where God has given counsel on this very topic.

When everything is going our way, patience is easy to demonstrate. The true test of patience comes when our rights are violated—when another car cuts us off in traffic; when we are treated unfairly; when our coworker or family member derides our faith, again. Some people think they have a right to get upset in the face of irritations and trials. Impatience seems like a wave of holy anger. Christ, however, praises patience as a fruit of the Spirit (Galatians 5:22) which should be produced for all His followers (1 Thessalonians 5:14).

Patience reveals our faith in God's timing, omnipotence, and love.

Although most people consider patience to be a passive waiting or gentle tolerance, most of the Greek words translated as "patience" in the New Testament are active, robust words. Consider, for example, Hebrews 12:1 (ERV):

> *Therefore let us also, seeing we are compassed about with so great a cloud of witnesses, lay aside every weight, and the sin which doth so easily beset us, and let us run with patience the race that is set before us.*

Does one run a race by passively waiting for those not concerned with their time or gently tolerating cheaters? Certainly not! The word translated as "patience" is synonymous with the definition for "endurance." As those who follow the counsel of Christ, we run the race patiently by persevering through difficulties, even if we can't see the end from the beginning.

That being said, patience does not develop overnight. God's power and goodness are crucial to the development of patience. Colossians 1:11 (NIV) tells us that we are strengthened by Him to "great endurance and patience," while James 1:3–4 encourages us to know that trials are His way of perfecting our patience. Our patience is further developed and strengthened by *resting* (remember the chapter on letting go?) in God's perfect will and timing, even in the face of evil men who "succeed in their ways, when they carry out their wicked schemes" (Psalm 37:7, NIV). Our patience is rewarded in the end "because the Lord's coming is near" (James 5:7–8, NIV). Remember, as is always the case even when it may be indistinguishable, "The Lord is good to those whose hope is in him, to the one who seeks him" (Lamentations 3:25, NIV). Our Wonderful Counselor will help us as we work through the times in our lives when impatience seems to be the rule and not the exception.

We see in scripture many examples of those whose patience characterized their walk with Christ. James points us to the prophets "as an example of patience in the face of suffering" (James 5:10, NIV). He also refers to Job, whose perseverance was rewarded by what the "Lord finally brought about" (James 5:11, NIV). Abraham, too, waited patiently and "received what was promised" (Hebrews 6:15, NIV). Jesus is our model in all things, and He demonstrated patient endurance: "Who for the joy set before him endured the cross, scorning its shame, and sat down at the right hand of the throne of God" (Hebrews 12:2, BSB).

How do we display the patience that is characteristic of Christ? First, we thank God. A person's first reaction when experiencing hardship is usually "Why me?", but we learn from scripture that we are to rejoice in God's will (Philippians 4:4; 1 Peter 1:6), believing in Isaiah's counsel that His ways and thoughts are not our own, but indeed much higher and holier (Isaiah 55:8–9). Second, we seek His purposes. Sometimes God puts us in difficult situations so that we can be a witness. Other times, He might allow a trial for the sanctification of character or help us grow in ways that we couldn't if we were constantly in a state of comfort and ease. Remembering that His whole mission is to help us achieve eternal life (Moses 1:27) will help us in our furnace of affliction. Third, we remember His promises such as Romans 8:28 (NIV), which tells us that "all things God works for the good of those who love him, who have been called according to his purpose." The "all things" include the things that try our patience.

The next time you are in a traffic jam, betrayed by a friend, or mocked for your testimony, how will you respond? The natural response is impatience or anger which leads to stress, confusion, and frustration. Praise God that, as Christians, we are no longer in bondage to a "natural response" because we are new creations in Christ Himself (2 Corinthians 5:17, NIV). Instead, we have the Lord's strength to respond with patience and complete trust in His power and purpose. "To those who by persistence in doing good seek glory, honor and immortality, he will give eternal life" (Romans 2:7, NIV).

As was mentioned a few paragraphs ago in Hebrews 12:2, as we exercise patience in our lives, let us do as the Savior did and *look forward with joy* to what being patient will bring to us. Throughout His atoning sacrifice for all mankind, Christ could have very easily folded under the immense pressure He was feeling, and I'm sure He was tempted too, but instead, He chose to focus on the joy that was going to be a permanent part of His future as He stayed patient, trusted in His Father, and continued forward in trust and love for you and me.

Chapter 10

Jesus Counsels Those Who Are Prideful

The sin of pride is a heart attitude expressed in an unhealthy, exaggerated attention to self and an elevated view of one's abilities, accomplishments, position, or possessions. Pride has been called "the cancer of the soul," "the beginning of all sin," and "sin in its final form." Ten Hebrew words and two Greek words are generally used in the Bible to refer to it. Pride, in its sinful form, is the direct opposite of humility, a trait that is highly praised and rewarded by God.[14]

Throughout this chapter, I'm going to be using a lot more scriptural references than I have in previous chapters to emphasize the importance of this topic and the soul-destructive results it can have on us if misunderstood.

WHAT IS PRIDE?

Pride is not always expressed as a negative quality in scripture. It can carry a positive connotation of self-worth, self-respect, and self-confidence. The apostle Paul communicated a positive sense of pride when speaking to the believers in Corinth:

I have the highest confidence in you, and I take great pride in you. You have greatly encouraged me and made me happy despite all our troubles. (2 Corinthians 7:4, NLT)

Pride becomes sinful when it is excessively self-focused and self-elevating, taking an "I choose myself over God" mindset. This kind of pride is what most often appears in scripture and is referred to as a high or exalted attitude—the opposite of the virtue of humility.

Charles H. Spurgeon described pride as "an all-pervading sin." He said,

Pride is so natural to fallen man that it springs up in his heart like weeds in a well-watered garden . . . .. Its every touch is evil . . . .. You

may hunt down this fox, and think you have destroyed it, and lo! Your very exultation is pride. None have more pride than those who dream that they have none. . . . Pride is a sin with a thousand lives; it seems impossible to kill it.[15]

Synonyms for pride in scripture include "insolence," "presumptuousness," "arrogance," "conceit," "high-mindedness," "haughtiness," and "egotism."

In Hebrew, the concept of pride is often expressed figuratively with words that suggest height. An interesting expression in Greek refers to a person being "puffed up" or inflated with pride. Rather than having substance, the prideful person is filled only with air:

He must not be a recent convert, or he may become puffed up with conceit and fall into the condemnation of the devil. (1 Timothy 3:6, ESV; see also 1 Corinthians 5:2; 8:1; 13:4, ESV); Colossians 2:18, ESV)

WHY IS PRIDE A SIN?

Pride is viewed as a great sin and rebellion against God because it presumes to possess excellence and glory that belong to God alone.

The danger of pride is that most people are unaware of their pridefulness: "You have been deceived by your own pride" (Obadiah 1:3, NLT).

Pride is perilously deceptive: "Pride leads to disgrace, but with humility comes wisdom" (Proverbs 11:2, NLT). It gives way to conflicts and quarreling (Proverbs 13:10). Pride adversely affects one's speech (Malachi 3:13; Proverbs 6:17).

Proud people do not think they need to ask forgiveness from God or admit their faults with others because they can't admit or even recognize their sinful condition. As a result, pride also affects a person's attitude toward others, often causing them to look down on others as less worthy or less able. Prideful people treat others with contempt and cruelty: "Mockers are proud and haughty; they act with boundless arrogance" (Proverbs 21:24, NLT). Pride is at the heart of prejudice.

The greatest danger in the sin of pride is that it keeps our eyes on ourselves instead of on God Almighty.

PRIDE IN THE SCRIPTURES

In Romans 1:30 (NLT), Paul describes unrighteous people who will incur the wrath of God as "backstabbers, haters of God, insolent, proud, and boastful. They invent new ways of sinning."

The Pharisees and other Jewish leaders were some of the most prideful people in the scriptures, noted for how they mistreated and spoke down to those beneath their social level. Jesus said of them:

And they love to sit at the head table at banquets and in the seats of honor in the synagogues. They love to receive respectful greetings as they walk in the marketplaces, and to be called "Rabbi." . . . But those who exalt themselves will be humbled, and those who humble themselves will be exalted. (Matthew 23:6–7, 12, NLT)

Pride caused the downfall of King Uzziah, who dared to burn incense on the altar of incense and was struck with leprosy as his punishment from God (2 Chronicles 26:16). Hezekiah became proud of heart after the Lord healed him. His pride brought God's wrath not only against him, but also against all of Judah, and Jerusalem (2 Chronicles 32:25–26).

King Herod's pride in accepting the people's worship and refusing to give God the glory for his greatness brought judgment. God struck him with sickness, and he was eaten by worms (ouch!) and died (Acts 12:21–23).

Of the Prince of Tyre, the Lord said,

In your great pride you claim, 'I am a god! I sit on a divine throne in the heart of the sea.' But you are only a man and not a god, though you boast that you are a god. (Ezekiel 28:2, NLT)

Many Bible scholars believe this passage refers to the original fall of Satan, which is also mentioned in Isaiah 14:12–15 (NIV):

How you have fallen from heaven, morning star, son of the dawn! You have been cast down to the earth, you who once laid low the nations! You said in your heart, "I will ascend to the heavens; I will raise my throne above the stars of God; I will sit enthroned on the mount of assembly, on the utmost heights of Mount Zaphon. I will ascend above the tops of the clouds; I will make myself like the Most High." But you are brought down to the realm of the dead, to the depths of the pit.

King Solomon said, "Pride goes before destruction, a haughty spirit before a fall" (Proverbs 16:18, NIV).

In scripture, pride not only caused the ruin of individuals but also of nations. Israel became proud and forgot God. Ultimately, it was the sin of pride that caused the people of Israel and Judah to be cut off from the promised land of Canaan (Isaiah 3:16; Ezekiel 16:50; Hosea 13:6; Zephaniah 3:11).

Pride is one of the sins that will be widespread among people in the last days,

For people will love only themselves and their money. They will be boastful and proud, scoffing at God, disobedient to their parents, and ungrateful. They will consider nothing sacred. They will be unloving and unforgiving; they will slander others and have no self-control. They will be cruel and hate what is good. They will betray their friends, be reckless, be puffed up with pride, and love pleasure rather than God. (2 Timothy 3:2–4, NLT)

The Bible warns people to evaluate themselves honestly for the sin of pride:

Because of the privilege and authority God has given me, I give each of you this warning: Don't think you are better than you really are. Be honest in your evaluation of yourselves, measuring yourselves by the faith God has given us. (Romans 12:3, NLT)

Now that I've quite literally put the fear of God in you regarding pride, I want to end on a softer note.

Jesus loves you. Jesus cares about you. He asks us to let go of pride so that we can more fully experience His light and presence in our lives. When we give credit to the Being who literally provides us with the breath in our nostrils and the sun in the sky, we recognize that we are very much not in control. Yes, we put forth the effort, but the results are out of our hands. We need Him to provide for us. All the money, all the accomplishments, all the fame, all the glory—are His. He's simply allowed us to experience them so that we may acknowledge and point others towards the Source of all good things and every good gift.

In the words of John the Baptist, "He must increase, and I must decrease" (John 3:30, KJV). And, as often attributed to C. S. Lewis, "Humility is not thinking less of yourself, it is thinking of yourself less."

Chapter 11

Jesus Counsels Those Who Struggle with Self-Esteem

I'd like you to take a few seconds and really think about these questions regarding self-esteem.

- Do you like yourself?
- Do you respect yourself?
- Do you internalize what people say about you, especially if it's negative?
- Do you find fault with yourself more easily than you compliment yourself?
- Do you think that having self-esteem is the same as having an inflated ego or being prideful?
- Do you think the world would be a better place without you?

Your answer to these questions can give you a pretty good indicator of whether or not you have a healthy amount of self-esteem in your life.

Growing up, I struggled with my self-esteem.

- I didn't like myself very much.
- I didn't respect myself.
- I often ruminated on negative things people said about me and to me.
- I found it much easier to hate on myself than love myself.
- I thought that if I was too confident or proud of myself for my accomplishments, I would be prideful and egotistical.
- There were moments when I thought the world would definitely be better without me.

I knew of a girl in high school who also struggled with her self-esteem. I won't use her name or personal details, but I will tell her story. She was raised in a Christian family with two parents who tried to instill good values, good morals, and the power of righteous living into her. She had dreams of becoming a pastor like her father and serving God through service to others. Her vision for her future was bright and her self-esteem was healthy.

Then, one day her life changed forever.

She went to a party with some of her friends and as she walked out to her car to retrieve her driver's license, she ended up being mugged and brutally raped by a man. It turned her world upside down.

Everything she thought she knew about herself, her potential, and her hopes for the future came crashing down. She felt violated. She felt like damaged goods. She felt ashamed . . . like it was *her* fault this had happened. She felt like her future was no longer bright, but very dark. Sixteen years of self-esteem built by those who loved her was destroyed in a matter of minutes by someone with nothing but a filthy desire to hurt, control, and manipulate someone else for their own selfish gratification.

Because her self-esteem and self-worth were decimated by the trauma inflicted upon her, she decided that life as she knew it wouldn't be worth living. She didn't kill herself physically, but emotionally, spiritually, and mentally she "died."

She didn't tell her parents what happened for fear they would be judgmental and turn her away from them because of their religious standing. She started filling the void the abuse left in her by being promiscuous with other boys and participating in substance abuse. She would put ads out on the internet for men to come to have sex with her, went to parties where she could use drugs and alcohol, and got into stripping.

One day when she was dancing at a strip club, a man walked up to her and offered her more money to come star in pornographic videos for a living.

She responded, "Sign me up!"

The next ten years of her life were filled with thoughtless exploitation, countless drug overdoses, numerous attempts to take her own life by way of suicide, and dozens of people claiming to "love" her, while only being interested in her as an object. She appeared like she was enjoying the life she was living, and the "career" she was pursuing, but deep within her soul ached with regret, longed for *real* love, and hoped for healing. In her own words, "I would fall asleep with a bottle of alcohol in one hand, and the money [I had earned that day] in the other. The money was the only thing keeping me going."

All this, because of a shattered sense of self-esteem.

Though tragic, her story ends with restitution, forgiveness, and *true* love.

After a couple more years in the industry, she finally had enough. She called her parents one day and asked for help. Instead of being judgmental (like she thought they would be), her parents reached out to her with arms of love, kindness, and compassion. They promised they would help her clean up her life if she would seek professional help for her sex, drug, and alcohol addictions.

Fast-forward to today, and this individual is ten years sober, working to pay off debts, and has a strong relationship with her parents. Her dream is to be a wife and a mother. Her self-esteem has been recovered from the piecemeal dissipation it used to be.[16]

I know parts of that story were difficult to read, but the moral is this: when it comes to creating a future for ourselves that is bright, hopeful, and fulfilling, having a healthy sense of self-esteem may be the greatest contributing factor. If we don't like ourselves, if we don't respect ourselves, if we act in a way that we *know* goes against our core beliefs and standards, we are unintentionally crafting a life of pain, poor choices, and regrets that will ultimately lead to sorrow.

What is self-esteem?

Simply put, it's how we regard ourselves. Regardless of the status of our mental or emotional health, the decisions we've made, or what has been done to us, if we wish to have healthy self-esteem, we need to live in accordance with what we know in our hearts and souls to be right.

When we *know* we are living a life true to our values, regardless of what external circumstances are swirling around us, we will be at peace with ourselves.

Jesus has given us counsel on this very subject throughout scripture.

When we feel like our self-esteem is lacking, the best course of action we can take is to go to the Being who gave it to us in the first place. By repenting of our sin and believing in Jesus Christ as our Lord and Savior, we are reconciled to the Father. The self-esteem damaged by our sin is regained and surpassed through faith in the righteousness of Christ. As believers in Jesus, we can always have a healthy sense of self-esteem because:

1. All human beings are made in the image of God and therefore are of value (Genesis 1:26–27; Psalm 129).

2. God loves us and has restored us (Ephesians 2:4–7).

3. Jesus died for us and has become the advocate with the Father toward us (Romans 5:8).

4. God redeemed us from slavery to sin and has empowered us to pursue holiness (Romans 6:17–18).

5. God has given us the opportunity to return to His presence (Colossians 1:13–14).

6. God is our friend (Romans 5:10).

7. We are heirs of God and co-heirs with Christ (Romans 8:16–17).

8. We have been uniquely gifted a mission in life to accomplish God's purposes (Romans 12:3–8).

We learn from these verses that the true basis of our self-esteem is not to be found in the things of this world but in our right relationship with God, which is made possible only through faith in Jesus, and through the gifts bestowed on us by Him. In Christ and because of Christ, we are of infinite worth to God. Unlike the ever-fluctuating self-esteem of the world, our worth does not and cannot change, for it is rooted in the love of Christ.

As Romans 8:35, 37–39 (KJV) so beautifully states,

Who shall separate us from the love of Christ? Shall tribulation, or distress, or persecution, or famine, or nakedness, or danger, or sword? . . . Nay, in all these things we are more than conquerors through him who loved us. For I am persuaded, that neither death, nor life, nor angels, nor principalities, nor powers, nor things present, nor things to come, nor height, nor depth, nor any other creature, shall be able to separate us from the love of God, which is in Christ Jesus our Lord.

Chapter 12

Jesus Counsels Those Who
Feel Isolated

A New York City taxi driver arrived at the final stop for his shift. He honked. After waiting a few minutes, he honked again. Because it was his last stop, he considered pulling away. Instead, he put the car in park and walked up to the door.

He knocked.

He heard an elderly voice, "Just a minute."

He then heard the shuffling of bags moving across the floor. Then the door opened.

It was a small woman in her 90's with a soft smile wearing a print dress and a pillbox hat with a veil pinned on it. As she answered, the taxi driver caught a glimpse inside the house. It looked as if no one had lived there for years. All the furniture was covered in sheets, no clocks on the wall, and no knickknacks on the counters.

"Could you carry my bag?" the lady asked.

The cab driver walked her slowly down the steps of the front porch to the cab.

Once in the cab, the lady handed the driver an address and asked, "Could you drive through downtown?"

"It's not the shortest way," the driver answered.

"I'm in no hurry. I don't mind," she said. "I'm on my way to hospice . . ."

The driver and passenger shared a quick glimpse in the rearview mirror, enough for her to see his concern and continue:

"I don't have any family left. The doctor says I don't have very long."

The driver quietly reached over and shut off the meter then asked, "What route would you like me to take?"

For the next two hours, they drove through the city. She showed the driver where she once worked, the neighborhood where she and her husband first lived, a furniture warehouse that had once been a ballroom when she was a girl. There were a few parts of town she asked the driver to slow down, and she would sit, staring into the darkness, saying nothing.

After a couple hours, she suddenly said, "I'm tired. Let's go now."

They drove in silence to the address she had given him. When they arrived, two nurses came out to the cab as soon as they pulled up. They must have been expecting her.

The driver opened the trunk to take out the suitcase. As he shut the trunk, she was already in a wheelchair.

"How much do I owe you?" she asked, reaching into her purse.

"Nothing," said the driver.

"You have to make a living," she answered.

"There are other passengers," he responded.

Almost without thinking, the driver bent and gave the lady a hug. She held on tightly.

"You gave an old woman a little moment of joy," she said. "Thank you."

The driver gave a final squeeze of the lady's hand and the two turned to go their separate ways. As he got in the car and glanced over to her, the door was shut.

He didn't pick up any more passengers that night. In fact, he could hardly speak.

What if that woman had gotten an angry, self-centered, or impatient driver? What if she got someone who refused to get out and go to her door? Refused to take the time driving around the city?

The taxi driver couldn't shake the feeling that this single moment may be one of the most important moments of his life.[17]

There may be times in your life when you feel like this older lady at the beginning of the story: forgotten, unaided, uncared for, and seemingly inadequate. You may be old, you may be young, you may live alone, or you may be surrounded by family or acquaintances. We all have times in our lives where no matter who is around us, we can feel isolated. Regardless of when those moments arise, the lonely cries from the foxholes of your heart are heard. The tears you shed in your moments of vulnerability and pleading are seen. They're seen and heard by our Wonderful Counselor—the individual who knows the workings and intents of every human heart. He's coming for you. He's going to send you your very own cab driver to offer you a moment of respite. A moment of "I see you," and "You're not forgotten."

Jesus understands isolation. He understands feeling abandoned, deserted, unaccompanied, and forlorn. He knows what it's like to be constantly in the public eye yet feel invisible. Though part human, His true nature was that of Divinity.

Can you imagine how isolated you would feel at times knowing your true identity and where you came from and the power you possessed, yet living in world of conflicts, deadlines, and small-mindedness brought on by apostles and pharisees alike?

In the words of Matthew 6:30 (KJV), Jesus Himself proclaims, "O faithless and perverse generation, how long shall I be with you? how long shall I suffer you?"

Whether you're reading this book in 2023, 2025, or 2055, throughout the world, we've just gone through multiple years of a global pandemic that brought governments, hospitals, and individuals to their knees. Within a matter of weeks, schools, shopping centers, churches, and airports were shut down. Some were abandoned in faraway countries. Others were subject to complete isolation in their homes or apartments for days, weeks, or sometimes months without outside interaction with family, friends, or pets. Everyone you knew was on high alert, wearing masks, social distancing, and dealing with the uncertainty of the future.

The social and emotional destruction this reaped on people across the world will have repercussions for years to come.

Reports of anxiety increased to 50 percent and depression to 44 percent by November 2020—rates six times higher than 2019—according to a new report in the journal *Translational Behavioral Medicine*.[18]

Among adults in America aged 18–29, the impact on mental health was even more severe. Rates of anxiety and depression increased to 65 percent and 61 percent, respectively, of the respondents in that age group, according to the report.

Where do we turn for peace? Where do we look for comfort, understanding, and a feeling of belonging?

Among family, friends, therapists, pets, doctors, or nature, the arms of Jesus should be the first place.

As He said, "Seek ye first the kingdom of God, . . . and all these things shall be added unto you" (Matthew 6:33, KJV).

What are all these things? That's the beautiful part. It all depends on your individual circumstances.

What do you desire at this very moment? Guidance? Peace? Love? Understanding? Empathy? Knowledge? Forgiveness?

They can all be found by seeking *first* the kingdom of God . . . by seeking Jesus Christ, the Son of God. For because He is the giver of every good gift, He knows perfectly how to bestow upon each of us depending on our individual circumstances *exactly* what we need and when we need it. Go to Him first, through whatever medium you best feel you can communicate and hear His word—then stand still, fear not, and believe—He will come to your aid.

It may be through a taxi driver like the old lady experienced, a random text from a friend, an out-of-the-blue encouraging quote on your Instagram/Facebook feed, a smile from a stranger, a song from a bird, or an unexplainable feeling of warmth and security that seems to envelop you like a hug.

The crushing feeling of isolation will be lifted. The sun will rise. The clouds will part.

As you seek Him and pay attention to seeming "coincidences" or random happenstances, you'll notice that they weren't coincidences at all, but a love note sent directly to you from the Wonderful Counselor Himself.

ALL AGENCY
PARTY
SEPTEMBER 8, 2023

Chapter 13

...ounsels Those Who
...ow Their Life's Purpose

...in life?

...e moment or another we've all heard or read this
...e known since they were eight years old exactly
...whether that was conducting symphonies, paint-
...neless, or playing professional sports. For others,
...they've read, or how many people they've talked
...len . . . almost undetectable.

...rpose with purpose. The scriptures undeniably

*...orkmanship, created in Christ Jesus for good
...red beforehand so that we would walk in
...KJV)*

In short, you are the solution to a problem, and becoming that solution is your purpose.

The challenge isn't always knowing if you have a purpose. It's discovering what your purpose is that can feel mysterious and at times a bit overwhelming.

So, how do we discover what our purpose in this season of our life is, let alone our entire life?

Here are a few questions you can ask yourself that may help lead you toward the answer.

What would you do with your life if you knew you couldn't fail?

It's the first question I ask people who are struggling to discover their purpose. Fear of failure is by far the greatest obstacle that keeps us from discovering and walking in our purpose.

I've watched people struggling with this fear drown themselves in an ocean of "*what ifs.*"

What if I leave my job and the business I want to start falls through?

What if the seed I plant doesn't grow?

What if the degree program that I feel passionate about turns out to be too difficult and I can't graduate?

The "*what if*" question may take on a lot of different forms, but the source is the same—it all goes back to a fear of failure.

When it comes to pursuing your purpose, the most devastating thing that could happen to you is not failure. The most devastating thing that could happen is for you to become successful at the wrong thing.

What in life bothers you the most?

The reason something bothers us is often that our purpose in life is to help fix that problem.

In the Bible, it bothered Nehemiah that the wall around Jerusalem was broken down. Why? Because repairing that wall was a part of his purpose.

It bothered Moses that the nation of Israel was in Egyptian captivity. Why? Because it was Moses's purpose to lead those people to freedom.

It bothered Jesus's disciples that the crowd of 5,000 men who came to hear Jesus teach were hungry and there was nothing to eat. Why? Because Jesus intended to use this moment to teach His disciples that the reason it bothered them was because He was going to work through them to fix it!

So, let me be your life coach for a moment: what bothers you?

Sex trafficking? Addiction? Homelessness? World conflict? A lack of leadership in our culture? Watching young couples struggle in their marriage? Maybe empty seats in church bother you, or people not knowing how to handle their money?

The reason something bothers you may very well be because God created you to become the solution to that problem.

How have the struggles you've endured impacted your life?

Purpose is often born out of adversity.

Where you've come from is often a clue to what God's calling you to.

Jesus took Peter from catching fish to being a fisher of men.

Jesus took the Apostle Paul from persecuting the church to building the church.

Joseph was sold as a slave and betrayed by his brothers, but he was carried away to the very nation that he would eventually lead.

So, how has what you've been through impacted your life?

What would you do with your life if you knew your family would support your dream unconditionally?

Sometimes we dismiss our true purpose because we don't believe we would have the support of the people closest to us.

I've talked to men and women alike who knew exactly what they were passionate about but couldn't muster the courage to pursue it because they didn't feel like they had the support of their families. I've sat and talked with college students who felt trapped because they were pursuing the degree that their parents wanted them to have rather than the one they felt called to.

At this point in the discovery process, I want you to imagine receiving the full support of the most important people in your life, even if you don't think they'd give it to you. This might help you uncover another clue to discovering your true purpose.

What would you do with your life if you knew that you wouldn't have to face the pain of dealing with your past?

Sometimes the most intimidating obstacle standing between us, and our purpose is our fear of having to deal with the pain of our past.

We often want to pursue our purpose, but we don't want to have to dig through the baggage of yesterday to do it. If that's you, then listen to me very closely: *as long as your fear of the process is greater than your frustration with your progress, you'll never fulfill your purpose.*

The good news? You're not alone. God will give you what you need to overcome your past so that you can walk in your purpose. Deuteronomy 31:6 (NKJV) says,

> *Be strong and of good courage, do not fear nor be afraid of them; for the Lord your God, He is the One who goes with you. He will not leave you nor forsake you.*

What comes easy for you that doesn't come easy for your friends or family?

We often overlook the things that we already do really well. This is why everyone can find benefit in going to therapy or finding a life coach—someone who can see the gifts in you that you can't see in yourself.

These things often come so naturally that we never stop to consider the fact that they might really be supernatural.

We assume that because it comes easy for us, it must be common and therefore easy for others also, but that's not always true. Not everybody can work with computers, people, money, or business the way you can. Not everyone can draw or take photographs as you can. Not everybody can organize their life as easily as you, cook as well as you, listen as well as you can, or make a house into a home the way you're able to. Sometimes the treasure of our purpose is hidden in plain sight. 2 Corinthians 4:7 (KJV) says it like this: "we have this treasure in earthen vessels . . ."

So, take a minute and take stock of your life. What do you do that hardly takes any effort to produce results? What do you do that you can make look easy? You may be surprised to discover how much treasure God's buried inside of you.

Don't take what God's already equipped you to do well for granted. It may indeed need some polishing and development, but even in its rawest and most undeveloped form, it can be another clue that will help lead you to your purpose.

What are you willing to sacrifice for?

This is a big one. Sometimes in order to hone in on your purpose, the question you need to ask yourself isn't, "What am I trying to get?" but rather, "What am I willing to give up?"

Jesus repeatedly said "no" to what appeared to be great opportunities so that He could put Himself in a position to fulfill His purpose. And when it comes to sacrifice, Jesus led the way. Hebrews 12:2 (NASB) says,

> *Jesus . . . who for the joy set before Him endured the cross, despising the shame, and has sat down at the right hand of the throne of God.*

Jesus was willing to sacrifice what looked like "good opportunities" on the front end to fulfill His ultimate purpose on the back end.

Discovering and developing your purpose will require seasons of sacrifice. You'll have to say "no" to a *good thing* now in order to say "yes" to a *great thing* later. And not everyone will understand or agree with the decisions you make when you get serious about pursuing your purpose.

So, what are you willing to sacrifice for? The answer to this question may very well be a clue that leads you to your purpose.

What would you do with your life if you knew money wasn't an issue?

Sometimes we allow limited resources to put limits on our purpose.

Personally, I believe that if it's God's will, it's God's bill. God doesn't need what you don't have in order to fulfill His plan for your life.

I once heard a quote that said,

> *God never gives you a dream that matches your budget. He's not checking your bank account; he's checking your faith.*

It's been my observation that a lot of people miss their purpose by putting the wrong priority on money either by focusing on the presence of it or the lack of it. In fact, the Bible says:

> *. . . some people, craving money, have wandered from the true faith and pierced themselves with many sorrows. (1 Timothy 6:10, NLT)*

Remember—there's nothing wrong with making money or having money. Just make sure money doesn't have you. Bishop Dale Bronner may have said it best,

> *You don't have to choose between God and money, you just have to choose which one you're going to serve.[19]*

One of the worst mistakes people make is choosing to pursue a paycheck rather than pursue their purpose. That's backward. If you pursue your purpose, the paycheck will eventually pursue you. Never allow what you don't have now to prevent you from becoming who you will be later.

What in life are you naturally passionate about?

What do you spend your time thinking about, talking about, reading about, watching, or listening to?

Our passions and interests are often times put there by God Himself as a means of pointing you towards your purpose. Psalm 37:4 (KJV) says that if you'll delight yourself in the Lord, ". . . He will give thee the desires of thine heart." That doesn't mean that God will give you whatever you want, it means that He'll put the proper desires in your heart to pursue His will and purpose for your life.

Here's something for you to consider:

Your Gifts + Your Passion = Your Purpose.

If you had ten extra hours per week that you could spend on anything, how would you invest those extra hours?

The reason we often won't pursue our purpose is that we keep telling ourselves, "I don't have time."

I don't have time to write that book.

I don't have time to work on a business plan.

I don't have time to launch that blog or website.

I don't have time to go back to school, read a book, serve in ministry, find a mentor or life coach, or get my vision for my life or family down on paper.

But the truth is, we make time for things that matter to us the most.

Time is your most valuable resource. The way we invest it will determine what we get back out of it. Your answer to this question may help uncover what you're truly passionate about and you may need to restructure your days in order to make time to work on your purpose. Once you discover your answer to this question—make up your mind to make up your mind! No more excuses. Carve out and protect some time each week to work on discovering, developing, and protecting your God-given purpose.

Chapter 14

Jesus Counsels Those Who Feel Crushed

We all know the feeling. Too many deadlines. Too few resources. Gas prices are too high . . . our salary is too low. Kids are starting to distance themselves from us . . . our marriage relationship is starting to feel like we're just roommates. The illness has spread, and the medication isn't working fast enough.

Whatever our circumstances may be, we all have the occasion to feel crushed. Buried. Covered. Weighed down. It's like we're gasping for air as the ocean waves crash down upon us. We get little moments of relief, but the overall experience leaves us more drained and downtrodden than relieved.

We need help.

We need assistance.

We need someone to come to our aid.

You may recall that when Christ atoned for our sins, He spent quite a few hours in the Garden of Gethsemane. Why was He there? Perhaps one reason is because of what the garden symbolized; as it was filled with olive trees, trees that were used to make olive oil. To produce olive oil in Jesus's time, olives were first crushed by rolling a large stone over them. The resulting "mash" was placed in soft, loosely woven baskets, which were piled one upon another. Their weight expressed the first and finest oil. Then added stress was applied by placing a large beam or log on top of the stacked baskets, producing more oil. Finally, to draw out the very last drops, the beam was weighted with stones on one end to create the maximum, crushing pressure.

I think of Matthew's account of the Savior as He entered Gethsemane that fateful night—that He "began to be sorrowful and very heavy."

And he went a little further, and fell on his face, and prayed, saying, O my Father, if it be possible, let this cup pass from me: nevertheless not as I will, but as thou wilt. (Matthew 26:39, KJV)

Then, as I imagine the distress grew even more severe, He pleaded a second time for relief and, finally, perhaps at the peak of His suffering, a third time. He endured the agony until justice was satisfied to the very last drop. This He did to redeem you and me.

To those who are currently being crushed . . . know that you're in good company. Heavenly company. Divine company. Your Counselor knows *exactly* what you are feeling. He comprehends your deepest fears, your greatest challenges, and your darkest secrets. The God who knows your name empathizes with and wants to help you—as He did with other children who were going through similar times of crushing.

One could argue that Job went through the most suffering of any figure in scripture other than Jesus Himself. God allowed Satan to buffet Job to such a degree that he started to despair even of life and the day of his birth. His friends accused him of sin, his wife told him to curse God and die, and Job never did find out the reason why God allowed him to suffer so much loss. He lost his children, his wealth, his health, his crops, his livestock, and even the relationship of his wife and best friends who turned on him and accused him of suffering because of his sins.

Job felt like He was God's enemy due to his suffering (Job 13:23–24) and started complaining to God about his condition (Job 23:3–4). Make no mistake about it, Job really struggled with his suffering, saying,

I loathe my very life; therefore I will give free rein to my complaint and speak out in the bitterness of my soul. I say to God: Do not declare me guilty but tell me what charges you have against me. Does it please you to oppress me, to spurn the work of your hands, while you smile on the plans of the wicked? (Job 10:1–3, NIV)

Have you felt this too? Have you asked these same questions? If so, you are not alone. God understands. He knows our frame and that we are all frail, feeble, and weak, made of dust (Psalm 103:14). It's okay to question God and doubt Him but we don't need to stay there. After God answered Job (Job 38, 39), he repented and was humbled before God (Job 42).

Jeremiah is known as the weeping prophet. Jeremiah was called by God around 626 BC. and was one of the most tenderhearted prophets that Israel ever had. His heart broke for the nation that refused to listen to God's words given through him. They rejected every single word of his prophecies and listened to those who gave good news, even though it turned out to be false (Jeremiah 43).

Jeremiah knew that these false prophets were only saying what the people wanted to hear, much like the modern, watered-down gospel that is being preached from behind many pulpits today. Jeremiah's mission was to turn the nation of Judah toward repentance and to rid the nation of idolatry that had spread throughout the land. Sadly, God had already told Jeremiah that the people wouldn't listen to him and would be sent into captivity (Jeremiah 7:27; 14:12).

There was nothing that Jeremiah could do to persuade the people, and this made him lament even more over the nation's rebellion toward God. There was no shortage of naysayers lined up against Jeremiah and his life was sought after frequently (Jeremiah 11:21–23). More than once they tried to stone him to death (Lamentations 3:53). Jeremiah was grieved over the persecution that his prophecies caused, and he became a laughingstock and the target of frequent mocking (Jeremiah 20:7), but he knew that he couldn't keep God's words to himself (Jeremiah 20:9) even if it meant long-term imprisonment (Jeremiah 37:16).

Once "they took Jeremiah and cast him into the cistern of Malachiah, the king's son, which was in the court of the guard, letting [him] down by ropes. And there was no water in the cistern, but only mud, and Jeremiah sank in the mud" (Jeremiah 38:6, ESV). If anyone faced a hopeless struggle, it was Jeremiah, but even though he faced such a trial, he knew God would deliver him someday and knew that He would prosper him, and this gave him hope (Jeremiah 29:11).

You're not alone.

You can make it through these difficult times.

Though you cannot see around the corner of your adversity, your Wonderful Counselor can. Turn to Him and allow Him to work with you through your darkest times.

Finally, I want to close out this chapter by reminding you that you can see your challenges in one of two ways—that they're there to destroy you, or that they're there to help you realize your fullest potential. It's all about having perspective be your power . . . not your prison.

You may feel buried at this time in your life . . . but I think you're being planted instead. There is little difference in the motion of planting and burying. If you asked a seed how it felt about being planted, it would probably tell you it feels like it's being buried. It feels dark, lonely, and forgotten. But remember, seeds aren't planted with the purpose of being suffocated, crushed, or killed. They're planted with the purpose of rising higher than they've ever dreamed or imagined.

So are you. You're being planted. And soon, you'll see the light again as you break through the soil and come to grasp your purpose and potential in life.

Chapter 15

Jesus Counsels Those Who Are Tempted

It's late at night, you've been under stress all day, and you start to feel the urge. The urge to smoke. The urge to drink. The urge to view pornography. The urge to binge eat. The urge to curse. The urge to drown your tension in something that will feel good at the moment but will ultimately leave you with more pain and sorrow in the long run.

What do you do? Too often, with myself included, we take the easy way out. We go for the momentary pleasure. We reach for the temporary relief . . . only to be disappointed. We're not truly relieved. We're not really satisfied.

Jesus never sinned but He did face temptation. In Hebrews 2:18 (KJV) we read,

For in that he himself hath suffered being tempted, he is able to succor them that are tempted.

Jesus is the only person who lived a sinless life. Peter wrote of Jesus,

Who did no sin, neither was guile found in his mouth.
(1 Peter 2:22, KJV)

Even though He lived a sinless life, He did not live without temptation.

For we have not an high priest which cannot be touched with the feeling of our infirmities; but was in all points tempted like as we are, yet without sin. Let us therefore come boldly unto the throne of grace, that we may obtain mercy, and find grace to help in time of need.
(Hebrews 4:15–16, KJV)

Jesus understands the feeling of being tempted. He knows the pull, the tug, the urge, the desire, the impulse. And, more importantly, He understands how to overcome. How to move past. How to stand strong.

We may all be aware that following His baptism by John the Baptist and as a preparation for His public ministry, Jesus fasted for forty days.

Yes, 40. No, not 40 hours, not 4 days, not 14 days . . . 40 days.

Now, I don't know about you, but when I go without food for even 12 *hours* I start to get hangry, impulsive, snippy, and start to lose control of my emotions . . . this is key ground for temptations to enter.

Jesus went without food for 40 days . . . and in that state of hunger, fatigue, and exhaustion (both physically and spiritually), the temptations came . . . and they came hard.

He was tempted by the adversary to inappropriately use His supernal power to satisfy physical desires by commanding that stones be made bread, to gain recognition by casting Himself down from the pinnacle of the temple, and to obtain wealth and power and prestige in exchange for falling down and worshiping the tempter (see Matthew 4:1–9)

David A. Bednar wisely noted of Jesus's exchange with the devil,

> *It is interesting to note that the overarching and fundamental challenge to the Savior in each of these three temptations is contained in the taunting statement, "If thou be the Son of God." Satan's strategy, in essence, was to dare the Son of God to improperly demonstrate His God-given powers, to sacrifice meekness and modesty, and, thereby, betray who He was. Thus, Satan attempted repeatedly to attack Jesus's understanding of who He was and of His relationship with His Father. Jesus was victorious in meeting and overcoming the strategy of Satan.*[20]

How was Jesus victorious?

He remembered who He was by quoting *Whose* He was. He used the words of His Father to counter the words of the adversary. Each time the devil lied to Him, Jesus responded with, "It is written," and quoted him the Word.

Let's discuss for a moment three lessons about temptation.

Being tempted is not a sin; giving in to temptation is sin. Those who are trying to honor God should never willfully put themselves in a position where they would face unnecessary temptation. One of the best ways to deal with sin is to stay away from it. You should fortify yourself against temptation with knowledge of God's Word. "Thy word have I hid in mine heart, that I might not sin against thee" (Psalms 119:11, KJV).

Being tempted does not mean that we must give in to sin. The same kind of temptation that you face has been both faced and resisted by others. Paul said they are "common to man.

There hath no temptation taken you but such as is common to man: but God is faithful, who will not suffer you to be tempted above that ye are able; but will with the temptation also make a way to escape, that ye may be able to bear it. (1 Corinthians 10:13, KJV)

We must remember that knowledge of the word of God and a love for it are the keys to resisting temptation in our lives just as it was in the life of Jesus.

Being tempted is something we will all face; let us stand boldly against the devil and have the courage to resist temptation. Matthew wrote, "Watch and pray, that ye enter not into temptation: the spirit indeed is willing, but the flesh is weak" (Matthew 26:41, KJV). In James 1:12 (KJV) we read, "Blessed is the man that endureth temptation: for when he is tried, he shall receive the crown of life, which the Lord hath promised to them that love him."

Remember, the goal of a follower of Christ is not to never feel tempted, but to process that temptation effectively and move past it.

As a certified life coach, I've spent hundreds of hours with various individuals helping them overcome negative habits and addictions in their lives—and one of the first things I try to help them understand is how the brain works when it comes to habits, addiction, and temptation.

First off, there are two areas of the brain that I'd like to focus on. The amygdala, and the prefrontal cortex.

The amygdala is part of the brain near the brain stem where we process a lot of our emotions, including fear, anxiety, pain, happiness, and excitement. Though there are many areas of the brain involved in emotion, the amygdala is one of the most prominent, and for the purposes of this information, it is the pleasure center of the brain when it comes to temptation.

The prefrontal cortex is home predominantly to our decision-making and problem-solving skills. When activated, we make healthy and smart decisions. When it's offline, we tend to make regret-worthy decisions.

When it's been a long day and we are hungry, tired, or stressed and we start to feel the urge to do something we know we shouldn't do (i.e. drink alcohol, smoke a cigarette, view pornography, binge eat our favorite dessert, etc), the prefrontal cortex shuts off and the amygdala lights up in our brain.

Our brains tend to always want to take the path of least resistance, and it's always easier to choose the urge than to try and do something else . . . but as was alluded to previously, the more we give in to temptation right when it comes up, the harder it becomes to withstand it in the future.

So, the question comes in, when we feel tempted to choose the easier wrong than the harder right, what do we do?

Well, in the spiritual sense, we ask for help. We pray. We ask God to send angels to our aid, and to preserve us from the devil's temptation.

Next, we take action ourselves.

One way to turn the prefrontal cortex on and extinguish the craziness of the amygdala is to write—and not just on our phone or on a laptop (though those can be viable options if pen/pencil and paper isn't near you), but in a journal. Why on physical paper? Because it's slower. When we take a bit longer to write out our thoughts, our brains process the information better. We think more deeply about what we are transcribing.

So, when you feel the urge, take out a piece of paper and write down these three questions:

1. What urge am I feeling? (Again, maybe to view pornography, smoke a cigarette, drink alcohol, binge eat dessert, etc.)
2. Why am I feeling it? (Am I hungry, tired, stressed, anxious, scared, nervous, etc.?)
3. What can I do instead of giving in to the urge? (If you're hungry, eat something. If you're tired, go to sleep. If you're stressed, exercise. If you're scared, phone a friend or say a prayer).

After you process the urge on paper, you'll feel in control. You'll realize that your brain is playing tricks on you. It is making you feel like you *need* whatever is tempting you, but in reality, what you really need is something else—you've just trained your brain to go for the temptation instead of the healthier option. Remember, your brain will always take the path of least resistance, so you need to retrain it into believing the choice that will reap the positive outcome is actually the path of least resistance because it will end up being better in the long run.

Ok, neuroscience lesson over. That being said, if you do struggle with urges and can't quite move past them, I'd love to help you. Email me at youngbandrew@gmail.com and we'll set up a time to talk.

To wrap up this chapter, I want to share my favorite quote from C. S. Lewis. It helped me (among other things) to overcome my temptations to view pornography in my teenage years, and I believe it can help you too:

No man knows how bad he is till he has tried very hard to be good. A silly idea is current that good people do not know what temptation means. This is an obvious lie. Only those who try to resist temptation know how strong it is; after all, you find out the strength of the German army by fighting against it, not by giving in. You find out the strength of the wind by trying to walk against it, not by lying down. A man who gives in to temptation after five minutes simply does not know what it would have been like an hour later. That is why bad people, in one sense, know very little about badness—they have lived a sheltered life by always giving in. We never find out the strength of the evil impulse inside us until we try to fight it: and Christ, because He was the only man who never yielded to temptation, is also the only man who knows to the full what temptation means—the only complete realist. [21]

Chapter 16

Jesus Counsels Those Who
Feel It's Too Late

Have you ever been told it's too late for you?
Too late to learn that instrument.

Too late to learn how to cook.

Too late to change that career path.

Too late to start exercising.

Too late to receive that miracle you've been praying for.

Too late to begin the transformation into who you know you can be.

John Pemberton invented Coca-Cola at 55

John Pemberton was a biochemist and American Civil War veteran best known for inventing Coca-Cola in 1886 when he was 55. He died two years later at the age of 57. Shortly before his death, John sold the formula to Asa Candler, who made Coca-Cola a household classic brand. Even though John Pemberton didn't get to live to see how much of a success his formula was, he still left his stamp on global history and culture.

Colonel Sanders began franchising KFC at 62

Colonel Sanders had a lifetime of experience with other businesses, but many of them failed. He was fired from many other jobs and had previous unsuccessful startups before KFC.

It wasn't until Sanders started cooking chicken that success began. The major problem was finding a distributor to sell his chicken. He went to over 1,000 distributors with his secret recipe just to get rejected. When all was seeming lost, the 1010 distributor finally said yes; he was 62. At 73 he sold KFC for 2 million dollars.

Today KFC's net worth is 15 billion. It is the second-largest fast-food industry right behind McDonald's with 22,621 locations globally in 150 countries.

Nelson Mandela—Prisoner to President at 76

As a young man, Mandela fought endlessly against the apartheid system in South Africa which was known for its racial discrimination and segregation between whites and blacks.

When Mandela was arrested and sentenced to life as a political prisoner in 1962, no one would ever imagine that he would ever see the outside of a cell ever again and be released, let alone become the country's first black president. Well, that's exactly what happened at the age of 76 after a change in the South African government. Mandela was released and replaced by the old regime that put him there.

Charles Darwin published "On the Origin of Species" at 50

Charles Darwin is renowned as the father of evolution, and it wasn't until he was 50 when he published his theories on evolution in his book, *On the Origin of Species.* This transformed the way we see the natural world with the belief that all species characteristics change over time due to their environment.

Henry Ford was 45 years old when he created the Model T car

The Ford Company was actually Henry Ford's third company, and his first success. The first two companies failed, and his third one struggled until they made the Model T. Model T was not their first try either. The nineteen earlier Ford models—A through S—all had major problems, including engines overheating and exploding. Model T changed the future of transportation forever, and Henry Ford was 45 at the time the car made it out of the assembly line.

Susan Boyle became a globally recognized singer at the age of 48

Few people made it through 2009 without hearing Susan Boyle's rendition of "I Dreamed a Dream" from Les Misérables—after all, it was one of the most-watched YouTube videos of the year (google it and be amazed). But what most people found extraordinary about the video, besides Boyle's obvious talent, was the fact that, at age 48, she had never sung professionally before. Boyle grew up enduring intense bullying and went on to work a kitchen job and take care of her parents after graduating. While she had always loved music and wanted to pursue it as a career, her familial duties held her back. But after making it to the final round of Britain's Got Talent in 2009, she landed a record deal and had the largest-ever sales debut for a female artist, eventually breaking global sales records—all in her late 40s.

Julia Child starting cooking at the age of 36

Starting an internationally successful culinary empire was hardly a lifelong goal of Julia Child's—in fact, Child was born in Pasadena, California in 1912 to a wealthy family and attended Smith College with the intention of becoming a writer. However, she met her husband Paul while working for the government during World War II, and the two moved to Paris. At the age of 36, Julia enrolled in the Le Cordon Bleu cooking school and soon after, with the help of her fellow students Simone Beck and Louisette Bertholle, formed her own cooking school: L 'Ecole de Trois Gourmandes.

Together the women wrote a revolutionary cookbook designed to make French cooking accessible to Americans called *Mastering the Art of French Cooking,* which remained a bestseller for five straight years after publication. An appearance on a Boston public television show to promote the book also launched a cooking show starring Child, which was eventually syndicated to 96 stations in America. Child, who hadn›t really shown interest in cooking until her mid-30s, was the first woman inducted into the Culinary Institute Hall of Fame in 1993 and received France›s highest honor, the Legion d'Honneur, for her work in 2000.

In the midst of doing research for this book, I discovered thousands of stories like the ones you just read, from people you've never heard of. It's not too late for you.

What about people in scripture who thought it was too late?

Well, an obvious first choice would be Sarah, the wife of Abraham, who had prayed for decades to have a child, thinking her childbearing days were long gone . . . until she was in her 90s. Biblical scholars inform us that Sarah was approximately 91, and Abraham 99 when their son Isaac was born.

God had a plan for them when they thought it was too late. Remember, God's time is not our time. His plans and strategies aren't dependent on a stopwatch, they're dependent on our faith, trust, and obedience when we don't get what we want.

Another example from the Bible pertains to a woman with the issue of blood (she's featured in an earlier chapter as well).

In Mark 5:21–34, we read of the lady with an issue of blood, who was healed when she touched Jesus's garments. This woman suffered from this issue for twelve years, unable to be relieved of the problem by doctors, and being forced to live on the outskirts of society. But at the sight of Jesus, she immediately believed she would be healed, so she pressed her way to reach Him and experienced a miracle.

It's not too late for you to be healed either.

Another example comes from John 5:1–15, in which we read about Jesus and the invalid, who was stuck at the poolside of Bethesda for 38 years. Having no one to carry him into the water to be healed, he sat and wasted away, feeling forgotten and abandoned . . . until Jesus came by. Jesus told him to rise and walk, and the man was immediately healed.

And what about Lazarus? Some would say he and his family were too late for a miracle . . . I mean, he died. And was buried. For days. Jesus was off doing other things when Lazarus's family was looking for him to heal their brother and son. As Jesus heard the news, He proclaimed in John 11 that Lazarus would be an example of the glory of God. Once Jesus arrived at the burial place, He commanded Lazarus to "come forth," and we all know the rest of the story.

What if God is making you wait because it will lead to His glory? What if by teaching you to wait and trust, He is letting "patience have her perfect work," as James 1:4 says?

It's never too late with God. Whether your miracle happens today, tomorrow, next month, next year, in 60 years, or after you've passed into His presence, keep trusting and keep believing. We know our Wonderful Counselor has our best interests in mind. He is good. He is the way-maker and the promise-keeper. He knows the timing. Seek His guidance and allow His peace to grace your path.

Chapter 17

Jesus Counsels Those Who Need to Repent

I love Jesus.

Truly, He is such an amazing God. He is good. He is kind. He is forgiving. He is merciful. He is just. He is compassionate. He is abundant. He is loyal. He is encouraging. He is loving.

And, for those who turn to Him and repent of their sins and shortcomings, He accepts and strengthens them.

In the words of Ezra Taft Benson,

Men and women who turn their lives over to God will discover that He can make a lot more out of their lives than they can. He can deepen their joys, expand their vision, quicken their minds, strengthen their muscles, lift their spirits, multiply their blessings, increase their opportunities, comfort their souls, raise up friends, and pour out peace.[22]

Our Wonderful Counselor is also our Great Physician, one capable of healing what we believe isn't healable, and forgiving what we believe is unforgiveable.

There's only one caveat—we need to accept His help. It's up to us to grab that outstretched hand of God and *allow* Him to take us as we are and increase our capacity to become better, holier, and healthier.

When Jesus Christ was on the earth, He shared a parable about repentance. In the parable, a Pharisee, a self-righteous religious leader, and a publican, a despised tax collector, both prayed at the temple. The Pharisee thought he had no need for repentance. He said, "God, I thank thee, that I am not as other men are, extortioners, unjust, adulterers, or even as this publican. I fast twice in the week, I give tithes of all that I possess" (Luke 18:11–12, KJV).

The publican, on the other hand, humbly prayed, "God be merciful to me a sinner" (Luke 18:13, KJV).

Jesus taught that the repentant publican, rather than the Pharisee, would be justified. Jesus taught that, "Every one that exalteth himself shall be abased; and he that humbleth himself shall be exalted" (Luke 18:14, KJV).

This parable beautifully captures Jesus's teachings about repentance. The society Jesus lived in measured righteousness by obedience to the law of Moses, a religious code that focused on outward performances.[23] But when Jesus came, He taught a higher law that emphasized our motivations and the desires of our hearts. Jesus taught that repentance has more to do with changing our hearts than it does with what is visible on the outside. He taught that we all must change and grow—we all must repent—to be acceptable before God.

The New Testament was originally written in the Greek language. In passages where the Savior calls upon people to repent, the word translated as "repent" is the Greek term *metanoeo*. This is a very powerful Greek verb. The prefix *meta* means "change." We also use that prefix in English. For example, the word *metamorphosis* means "change in form or shape." The suffix *noeo* relates to a Greek word that means "mind." It also relates to other Greek words that mean "knowledge," "spirit," and "breath."

In the words of Russell M. Nelson,

He invites us to change our minds, our knowledge, our spirit, even our breathing. For example, when we repent, we breathe with gratitude to God, who lends us breath from day to day. And we desire to use that breath in serving Him and His children. Repentance is a resplendent gift. It is a process never to be feared. It is a gift for us to receive with joy and to use—even embrace—day after day as we seek to become more like our Savior.[24]

In a letter to professor and vicar John Staupitz, Martin Luther wrote,

I learned that this word is in Greek metanoia and is derived from meta and noun, i.e., post and mentem, so that poenitentia or metanoia is a "coming to one's senses," and is a knowledge of one's own evil, gained after punishment has been accepted and error acknowledged; and this cannot possibly happen without a change in our heart and our love . . . Then I went on and saw that metanoia can be derived, though not without violence, not only from post and mentem, but also from trans and mentem, so that metanoia signifies a changing of the mind and heart.[25]

In Romans 12:2 (NIV), Paul reminds us,

Do not conform to the pattern of this world, but be transformed by the renewing of your mind. Then you will be able to test and approve what God's will is—his good, pleasing and perfect will.

Through metanoia, we seek God and His will in a changing of our hearts and minds.

Isn't Jesus such a good God? Isn't He so merciful and kind? Sometimes I can't believe it. How grateful we each should be that we aren't doomed to imminent and eternal damnation because of our sins.

There is always a way back. There is always a path to redemption.

Through Jesus's atoning sacrifice, the floodgates to mercy, forgiveness, and grace were opened—never to be closed again.

That being said, there are many out there reading this who believe that doctrine is sound for everyone else in their lives, but when it's applied to their own circumstances—it doesn't quite add up.

"I've gone too far," they lament.

"I've repented for the same thing hundreds of times . . . and yet I do it again," they cry.

"I've sinned too much," they weep.

Ok, let's pause for a moment, here. Who determined the limit on sin? Isn't sinning just one time, even in thought, "too much"?

The thoughts that arise when we believe that we've "gone too far" or "sinned too much" don't come from the Prince of Peace . . . they come from the prince of darkness, that slithering snake whose sole purpose is to make us doubt who we are (Psalm 100:3). Why does he attack our identity? Because he knows if he can get us to start doubting who we are, we will start looking to the world for answers. We will move outside of God, and when that happens, we're at the mercy of the adversary.

There is *always* a way back with Jesus. There is *always* another chance to repent and improve. Fall down 1,000 times and get up 1,001 times. God isn't disappointed in you. God doesn't hate you. God doesn't want to guilt-trip you. He wants you to come to Him and be healed. He wants you to come to Him and find peace. He wants you to come to Him and find your true self again.

Jesus told the prodigal son story in response to the Pharisees's complaint: "This man welcomes sinners and eats with them" (Luke 15:2, NIV). He wanted His followers to know why He chose to associate with sinners.

The story begins with a man who has two sons. The younger son asks his father for his portion of the family estate as an early inheritance. Once received, the son promptly sets off on a long journey to a distant land and begins to waste his fortune on wild living.

When the money runs out, a severe famine hits the country, and the son finds himself in dire circumstances. He takes a job feeding pigs. Eventually, he grows so destitute that he even longs to eat the food assigned to the pigs.

The young man finally comes to his senses, remembering his father. In humility, he recognizes his foolishness and decides to return to his father and ask for forgiveness and mercy. The father who has been watching and waiting, receives his son back with open arms of compassion. He is overjoyed by the return of his lost son.

Immediately the father turns to his servants and asks them to prepare an enormous feast in celebration of his son's return.

Meanwhile, the older son boils in anger when he comes in from working the fields to discover a party with music and dancing to celebrate his younger brother's return.

The father tries to dissuade the older brother from his jealous rage explaining, "Look, dear son, you have always stayed by me, and everything I have is yours. We had to celebrate this happy day. For your brother was dead and has come back to life! He was lost, but now he is found!" (Luke 15:31–32 NLT).

Remember, heaven is not filled with people who have never sinned. It's filled with those who have sinned, recognized their sin, taken responsibility for it, and turned to God for help.

Repentance isn't punishment. It's progress.

Repentance isn't meant to be scary. It's meant to be sacred.

Repentance isn't for failures. It's for those who wish to be more faithful.

Take your sins, shortcomings, and seemingly unforgivable actions to your Wonderful Counselor, and allow Him to guide you on the path that leads to love, peace, and holiness.

Chapter 18

Jesus Counsels Those Who Desire Peace

Peace.

The world needs it. Our families need it. Our souls need it. Our relationships need it. It seems like it's always out of reach. Conflicts, debates, wars, two sides pitted against one another—where can we turn for peace?

Isaiah referred to Jesus as the Prince of Peace (Isaiah 9:6). You know what that means, right? Heavenly Father is the King of Peace, and Heavenly Mother is the Queen of Peace. A throne of peace? You betcha. A place where we can turn when we need peace? 100%. A place guaranteed to offer us the peace our souls and the world yearns for? Without a doubt.

My favorite description of this peace God promises us is found in Philippians 4:7 (NHEB):

And the peace of God, which surpasses all understanding, will guard your hearts and your minds in Christ Jesus.

I can honestly say I've experienced that kind of peace. It would probably seem strange to the world, but it has been in the biggest struggles of my life that I discovered the most wonderful quiet inside my soul. In the midst of painful loss, it was as though heaven itself came down and wrapped me in a warm blanket of God's love and compassion.

How do we access this peace?

In the few verses preceding Philippians 4:7, there are actions to take that bring about the experience of peace that is so great, that we can't comprehend it. Those actions, per verses 4–6, are:

Rejoice in the Lord always.

Again, rejoice.

Let your gentleness be known to everyone.

(Because the Lord is at hand) Do not be anxious about anything.

Let your requests be made known to God by prayer and supplication with thanksgiving.

We have been empowered to have peace, and it seems to me it comes through faith. How can we "rejoice always," meaning also in difficult times, unless we have faith that God rewards those who diligently seek Him and will work things together for our good (Romans 8:28)? Isn't "rejoice always" an extraordinary statement? God instructs us to remain in a state of rejoicing throughout this thing called life.

We place aside the distractions and the conflict.

We humble ourselves.

We kneel down and look up.

We ask our Wonderful Counselor to provide us with the peace we desire.

And whatever you ask in My name, that I will do, that the Father may be glorified in the Son. (John 14:13, NKJV)

Therefore I tell you, whatever you ask for in prayer, believe that you have received it, and it will be yours. (Mark 11:24, NIV)

A story I heard once demonstrates this principle with precision:

Once there was a king who offered to give a prize to an artist who could best paint a depiction of peace. Many artists decided to participate and sent the king their masterpieces.

Among the various masterpieces, one picture was of a calm lake closely resembling peacefully towering snow-capped mountains where a blue sky with fluffy clouds was overheard.

The picture was exemplary. Most of those who viewed the paintings of peace from different artists thought that this painting was the best among all others.

But the king had another winner in mind. To the crowd's surprise, the picture that won was of a mountain too but was more plain and rugged than the other piece.

The sky was shady and looked angry because there was lightning. It was exactly the opposite of what peace should look like. The others thought that maybe the artist submitted a wrong painting showing a storm rather than peace.

What others didn't notice was that if you look closely at the painting, there is a tiny bush growing in the cracks of a rock. In the bush, there is a nest built by a mother bird and in the midst of the stormy weather, the bird sits peacefully on her nest.

In that specific portrait, it was depicted that in the presence of all the turmoil, there is still someone who can be calm in his or her heart.[26]

Many of us are familiar with the account in the book of Matthew where Jesus has recently finished preaching to a group of people and heads down to the sea in order to sail across to the other side. Without fail, His disciples followed Him (though I'm sure He wouldn't have minded a little alone time).

As the boat started its journey across the Sea of Galilee, Jesus fell quietly asleep. Within minutes a furious storm arose, and the boat was tossed violently on the waves. The disciples, many of whom were seasoned fishermen, must have been surprised by the severity of their situation because they yelled to Jesus, "Master, carest thou not that we perish?"

In other words, they probably couldn't believe that Jesus was asleep, and they were also terrified of their own lives being lost at sea.

Jesus, I'm sure a little upset that He was awakened from a much-needed (and deserved) snooze, stood and with authority spoke these three words, "Peace, be still."

As the words left His divine lips, the waves calmed, the wind rested, and the boat stood still on the water (Matthew 8:23–27, KJV).

How often do we find ourselves tossed to and fro with the storms of life?

How often do we call out to God, "Carest thou not that I perish?" Or, in other words, "Do you even care that this is so hard for me? Do you even care that I am struggling? Where are you, God?!"

I know I've repeated that plea many times over the course of my life. Through storms of mental illness, emotional turmoil, and deep uncertainty, my words echoed those of the disciples that stormy day on the Sea of Galilee.

And you know what?

He was there. My Wonderful Counselor heard me. He knew where I was. He knew what I needed. He knew how to help me. And just as He calmed the Sea, He calmed my heart. He calmed my anxiety. He calmed my fears. No, not necessarily right away. No, not necessarily the way I had hoped, but He calmed me in the way and at the time that I *needed*.

That's what He will do with you. He will take your storm and He will make it still. He has that power. In fact, He has *all* power. He can calm your situation just as easily and quickly as He can calm the Sea. After all, you're both made by Him for His purposes.

So, to those reading this who desire peace. To those reading this who can't seem to go one more hour with the pain they're carrying—go to your Wonderful Counselor and ask Him for peace. Ask Him to calm your troubled mind, your troubled heart, your troubled relationships, your troubled marriage, your troubled career, your troubled financial situation, your troubled mental health, and your troubled trauma.

He has promised He will not leave us comfortless (John 14:18).

Isaiah 32:17–18 (ESV) states,

And the effect of righteousness will be peace, and the result of righteousness, quietness and trust forever. My people will abide in a peaceful habitation, in secure dwellings, and in quiet resting places.

Rest in that peace, and that promise—and remember, our job is to put in the effort. It's God's job to produce the outcomes. That will require, at times, trusting His timing and His processes, but I promise it'll be for our ultimate benefit.

Chapter 19

Jesus Counsels Those Who
Need a Miracle

We've all been there.

The medical report isn't good.

The financial situation is bleak.

The relationship is struggling.

The future is unnerving.

We don't just need an encouraging word. We need saving. We need redemption. We need a way through this circumstance . . . We need a miracle.

What do we do when we need a miracle?

How do we act?

Where do we turn?

Whom do we trust?

If it's the world, we're going to be disappointed.

If it's Jesus, we're going to be at peace.

News about [Jesus] spread all over Syria, and people brought to him all who were ill with various diseases, those suffering severe pain, the demon-possessed, those having seizures, and the paralyzed; and he healed them. (Matthew 4:24, NIV)

Then [Jesus] arose and rebuked the winds and the sea, and there was a great calm. (Matthew 8:26, KJV)

Jesus had compassion on them and touched their eyes. Immed-iately they received their sight and followed him. (Matthew 20:34, NIV)

They saw Jesus approaching the boat, walking on the water. (John 6:19, NIV)

And as many as touched Him were made well. (Mark 6:56, NKJV)

Yes, we do serve a miracle-working God.

Verse after verse, story after story, instance after instance. Miracles so numerous that, were each occasion to be transcribed, "the world itself could not contain the books that would be written" (John 21:25, ESV).

The God who came that we may "have life more abundantly" is a miracle-working, miracle-loving, miracle-providing God (John 10:10, KJV). No, not just for the person on earth 2,000 years ago, or the neighbor down the street that you heard was healed, or that long lost cousin you don't know who could never conceive a child but *miraculously* did—no.

He is a miracle-producing God for *you*.

You may say to yourself, "That's great . . . but I've never experienced a miracle. Nope. Never."

Ok, perhaps you haven't been healed of cancer or received your sight after being blind, or instantaneously received the knowledge of all the answers on your physics test having not studied one minute . . . but I do know a miracle that happened in your life . . . a big one.

Jesus Christ suffered for you.

Jesus Christ atoned for you.

Jesus Christ died for you.

Jesus Christ rose from the dead for you.

Jesus Christ made it possible for you to be resurrected and live in an eternal state of glory and happiness.

And you know what? Even if you were the only person to ever live on this earth, He still would've done it for you.

Why? Because He loves you. He wants you to come home.

The miracle you're expecting or wanting may not be the miracle God knows you need at this time. And just to be clear, just because the miracle doesn't happen in your way and time *does not* mean that Jesus is not a God of miracles. Rather, it's up to you to be in a position of humility and faith where you can call on Him and ask for His help, but always with the mentality of "not my will, but thine, be done" (Luke 22:42, KJV).

Do you think Jesus asked for a miracle when He was bleeding in the Garden of Gethsemane?

Of course!

Did God deliver Him from His pain and remove the "cup" from Him right away (Luke 22:42–44, KJV)?

No.

Why? Because God knew Jesus needed the growth. God knew Jesus's mission. Even though it pained Him as Father to have to see His son suffering beyond measure, He knew what the outcome of it would be . . . the opportunity for all of His children to be able to come back home.

Similarly, when we pray for a miracle in our lives and don't receive it, even if we think it's the right thing for us and we find ourselves suffering, we can know that it's for a divine purpose that only Heaven understands.

Does God want you to be hurt?

No.

Does He want you to grow and learn and trust Him?

100%.

Sometimes the miracles of Jesus are performed within our ability to wait and trust, not in our ultimate deliverance from what is ailing us.

In the words of David A. Bednar, "Do you have the faith not to be healed?"[27]

Now, understanding that there are moments in life when we will not receive the miracle in our own way and time (but we still trust God regardless), there definitely are other moments when God blesses us with the miracle we need but weren't even aware of.

Think back on the moment when the car next to you on the freeway swerved rapidly and barely missed sending you into the off-ramp.

Think back on the moment when you were in bed with the stomach flu but felt a moment of reprieve as you said a brief prayer.

Think back on the moment when your first child was born.

Think back on the moment when you finally forgave that high school bully or that abusive partner.

Think back on the moment when you saw clearly what your life purpose was or understood how to achieve that goal you were seeking.

All these, and more, are miracles. They're divine instances of help, safety, security, prosperity, perspective, and grace.

In my opinion, we all experience anywhere between ten and one hundred miracles a day, they're just so ordinary to us that we don't recognize them.

How about the ability to breathe?

How about the ability to speak?

How about the ability to use your mind?

How about the ability to drink fresh water?

How about the ability to be free?

How about the ability to love?

How about the ability to choose our attitude?

How about the divine blessing of being forgiven for your sins?

I fully recognize that there may be someone reading this who can't relate to all those examples listed for one reason or another, but the general idea can be applied to any circumstance. What is something that you do every day that has become so routine to you that you may even disregard it as boring or no big deal?

It's those things that make up the majority of miracles in our lives.

Now, on occasion, we may be healed miraculously of an injury, experience a once-in-a-lifetime check on our doorsteps that helps us pay for our mortgage that month, or have our car start-up in the middle of nowhere even though it's out of gas . . . and those miracles are *awesome*. But the majority of what Jesus does is through the daily routines that we take for granted. It's in the little things. The tiny blessings. The unexpected tender mercies.

Take a moment and put this book down. Close your eyes, take out a piece of paper or simply relax. What is something that has happened to you today you can count as a miracle? What is something that has happened to you today you can see as a tender mercy from a loving Father? What is something that is happening to you *right now* that you can recognize and give credit to God for?

Ponder it.

Internalize it.

Give gratitude for it.

You're blessed and highly favored. You will receive healing. You will find peace. You will experience grace. You will see Jesus come through for you as your advocate, rescuer, redeemer, and perhaps most importantly, your friend.

Just think . . . if someone loves you enough to bleed and die for you, don't you think they love you enough to help you accomplish that goal, pay off that loan, redeem that relationship, and experience the peace that passes all understanding (Philippians 4:7)?

Jesus is a miracle worker . . . both the big ones, and the little ones . . . both the ones we notice, and the ones we don't . . . both the ones we pray for, and the ones we're blindsided by.

All of them. All the time.

He is a good God. He is a wonderful counselor. Turn your whole soul over to Him, plead for His help, offer your allegiance to Him, and trust that He knows best. One day it will all make sense, and you'll weep over the scar marks on His hands and feet with the utmost gratitude that He did it His way and in His time . . . even if it was different from yours.

Chapter 20

Jesus Counsels Those Who Feel Like Failures

In a world of filters and followers, it can seem like a daily battle *not* to feel like a failure. We've all seen the vacation pictures on Instagram that look too good to be true, or the gym bodies that seem too toned to be real, or the selfies that come across as too unblemished to be genuine. Regardless of how "fake" or "misleading" those pictures may seem at first glance if only for a moment, there are times when we may think to ourselves, "Wow, why can't my life be like that? Am I doing something wrong? Am I a failure?"

NO.

YOU.

ARE.

NOT.

What about that negative habit you're trying to kick? What about the pornography, the smoking, the swearing, the gossiping, the unkindness, the lying, or the drinking you're trying to overcome?

You will 100% have moments when you stumble . . . when you fall down . . . when you faceplant . . . when you relapse . . . when you fail.

But let's make one thing clear right here and now—there is a major difference between failing and being a failure.

Failing comes daily, sometimes hourly in our lives. We burn the toast, we yell at our kids, we stub our toes and say a "colorful" word, we forget to pay the power bill and see that we've been given a past-due charge. We never seem to live up to expectations, either our own or those of others . . . and when that happens, we often say to ourselves in defeat, "I'm a failure."

However, that's the wrong phrase to use and can inflict terrible things on our self-confidence and self-esteem.

You see, we are only failures when we give up . . . when we stop trying . . . when we choose to stay down instead of getting up one more time.

You are never a failure when you choose to look up and get up—and there's no one better to look up to than Jesus Christ.

"But Drew, Jesus never sinned . . . so how can He help me when I fail? How can He help me when I relapse for the 50th (or 500th) time?"

I've often had moments when these questions have entered my mind.

Something to think about is that I absolutely believe Jesus failed. Right, He never sinned, but I'm sure there were moments when He accidentally hit His thumb with the hammer in His carpentry shop, forgot to pay a tax, or got mad at His disciples when they were being stubborn. He probably failed thousands of times just like all of us, and hence "learned . . . by the things which he suffered" (Hebrews 5:8–14, KJV) how to succor us when we slip up.

When it came to sin, He didn't have to do it personally for Him to know what it was like—when He was in the Garden of Gethsemane and on the cross, He *literally* took on Him the sins of every single man, woman, and child who ever lived or would ever live on this earth (1 Peter 2:24). He felt the pain, regret, shame, anger, sorrow, sadness, grief, and disappointment that accompanies every sin.

He is the perfect individual to turn to regardless of how or when we fail in our lives.

Here's a story from my own personal life that you may be able to compare with a similar circumstance from yours.

As you may know from following me on social media or reading either of my previous books, *The Meaning of Your Mission*, or *Stand Guard at the Door of Your Mind*, I am very vulnerable and open about my own mental health journey. I believe that in sharing it, others will find hope, comfort, and relatability. Well, when I was nineteen and going through my very challenging and traumatizing battle with debilitating anxiety, depression, panic attacks, and bouts of suicide ideation, I met with a mental health professional who literally saved my life. He gave me the techniques to heal myself and prescribed me medication that bridged the gap in my ill brain and taught me that regardless of what had happened in the past, the future was bright and hopeful.

He inspired me to pursue the path of psychology and become a mental health professional myself, helping others heal and understand their own emotional and mental difficulties.

So, I went for it. I started studying neuroscience and psychology at the university I was attending and signed up for various chemistry and biology classes. As the classes progressed, I had a very real awakening that this material was too difficult for me to grasp at the present moment. I was still healing from my own mental infirmities, and the exhausting toll these science classes had on me was too much to handle . . . so I dropped out . . . not just out of the pre-med program, but out of college entirely.

I was lucky enough to have a full-time business opportunity come my way and decided that that was a better road for me to take than being scholastically (and mentally, and emotionally) crushed day in and day out.

Skipping forward, I worked for a leadership development company for four years, building my connections, learning about book publishing, podcasting, operations, marketing, sales, and management consulting, and made a good living for myself, my wife, and my daughter.

But, in 2021, I had the reoccurring thought that something was missing. I was providing well for my family, traveling, meeting amazing people, and working a lot from home—but I didn't feel fulfilled. I didn't feel like I was attending to my mission in life.

As I prayed and sought help from my Wonderful Counselor, the feeling of becoming a mental health professional kept coming back to my mind.

"I know I had that goal in my early twenties, but is it still good for me to pursue it?" I questioned.

"What about the great job I have now?"

"What about the opportunities I'd be giving up?"

"What will happen if I give up my salary and benefits to go into the unknown?"

These questions and many others filled the conversations my wife and I had for nearly a year as we wrestled with the proposition of giving up the safety and security of our current situation and trading it for the unknown with complete faith and trust in God, believing that He knew what we did not and could guide us in ways we couldn't imagine.

So, in August of 2022, I officially resigned from my full-time job, traded my paycheck for school loans (and some scholarships), bought a pack of pencils, a calculator, and a lot of textbooks, got my backpack out of storage, and went back to school in Fort Worth, Texas.

It was a rough first month. I failed . . . a lot. I failed a few quizzes in chemistry, a test in biology, and a couple of other assignments that I put in a lot of time and effort for. And for anyone who knows the process of being pre-med at a university and attempting to earn your way to admission into a graduate school, failing is *bad*. You do not want to fail! But, I was doing it constantly for the first month (or two!), and I didn't know why. I was even getting mad at God for having the *gall* to allow me to fail even though He saw me putting in the work, saying my prayers, and trying to do His will!

You see, I believed that by following God and putting my full trust in Him, I wouldn't fail. I thought that by doing His will, I would only see miracles, successes, and prosperity. But I learned that's not how it works. In doing God's will, we should still expect failures and weaknesses to abound, especially if we are doing something new or challenging. Why? Because in our failures, and in our weaknesses, God has plenty of room to act.

In our weaknesses, God's grace abounds.

In our failures, God's perfection arises.

In our humility, God's power amazes.

After that first month, I started to learn more effective and efficient ways of studying. I started praying for God to bless me with discernment, and to help me study the things that would be on upcoming quizzes and exams. I stopped complaining and started praising. And the results came. No, not A's on everything (or most things), but I did see improvement, and I did see God's hand guiding me.

God's guiding you too, friend.

Through your failures, you're learning humility, patience, and perseverance.

Through your failures, you're learning what works and what doesn't.

Through your failures, you're growing, progressing, and moving towards a higher and better expression of yourself.

No, doing God's will, putting God first, and striving to keep God's commandments will not remove the failures from our lives—but doing those things will make sure that we have and recognize His matchless power when failures come.

Fall forward.

Fail forward.

Then rise!

You're only a failure when you refuse to get up.

Remember, our Wonderful Counselor is with us just as much in the valleys as He is on the mountaintops.

Reach out to Him, thank Him, praise Him, and ask Him to *consecrate your failures*, so that you can learn from them, improve upon them, and reach your grandest potential in life!

In the words of Winston Churchill, "Never, never, never give up!"

Chapter 21

Who Shall Separate Us from the Love of Christ?

I hope this book has brought you closer to Jesus Christ. That was my intention behind writing it, and I thank Him for giving me the opportunity to do so. You've seen throughout these pages a God who is there for us. You've read stories, prayers, scriptures, and personal experiences of individuals who, like you, faced unfair, unkind, or unbelievable challenges in their lives.

Whether mental, emotional, spiritual, physical, relational, or intellectual, our Wonderful Counselor is there for us in our times of trouble.

That doesn't mean we won't have difficult moments or feelings of being abandoned. Rather, we will be sustained *during* the difficult and trying times. We will be given the strength to not give up.

As we wrap up our journey together, I want to offer you 26 reminders that you can take with you throughout your upcoming days, weeks, months, and years. For more weekly reminders, feel free to follow me on Instagram (@mrdrewbyoung), or check out my Facebook profile.

God isn't preparing the blessing for us. He's preparing us for the blessing. The blessing is already prepared. The path is already paved. God knows the end from the beginning. It's up to us to stay faithful to Him through the rough patches, through the wilderness, and through the unknown. He'll always lead us where we need to go and provide nourishment and peace along the way. As the scripture says, "He leads me beside the still waters" (Psalms 23:2, NKJV).

God finished you before He started you (Jeremiah 1:5).

He knows the plans He has for you (Jeremiah 29:11).

He is a good God (Psalm 103:8).

Life may be throwing you some struggles right now. You may be a single parent trying to make it. You may be grieving a loss of a loved one. You may be experiencing a conflict with a family member or friend that eats at you.

Whatever the question and whatever the difficulty—the answer is found in Jesus. His plan for us requires challenges so that we can learn to trust, obey, and overcome.

1. Your greatest mission in life will most likely come out of your greatest pain in life. God never uses anyone greatly until He tests them deeply. Your pain, your anxiety, your trauma, your sorrow, your fatigue . . . all of it.

    You're being prepared.

    You're being molded.

    You're being sculpted.

    Going through some of the toughest moments in my life has taught me this exact principle.

2. Some days you'll move mountains. Some days you'll move from the bed to the couch. Both are ok and necessary.

3. God is more concerned with our character than our comfort. I know that's hard to hear, but God wants us to grow . . . and He wants us to be fulfilled . . . and He wants us to be happy . . . but a lot of the time that only comes through experiencing hardship and struggle. If we go through struggles with God, He'll work all things together for our good.

    He loves us.

    He's a good God.

    He will strengthen us.

    "Trust in the Lord with all thine heart, and lean not unto thine own understanding. In all thy ways acknowledge Him, and He shall direct thy paths" (Proverbs 3:5–6, KJV).

    It doesn't say He "might" direct us . . . it promises us He *will*, as we go through all the difficult times.

4. God never promised that what we went through would be good. What He did promise is that He'll work everything together *for* our good (Romans 8:28). You may be going through something right now that isn't good. An illness. A bad relationship. Abuse. A poor financial situation. A stressful circumstance. A moment of grief. Whatever is going on in your life that isn't good, know that God will work it for your good as you continue in hope.

    He's a promise keeper.

He's a miracle worker.
He's a hope giver.
The light will come back.
The happiness will return.
The goodness will be manifested once again.

5. All of us at some point will go through a dark place—a sickness, a divorce, a loss, a child who breaks our heart. It's easy to get discouraged, give up on our dreams, and think that's the end. But God uses the dark places. They're part of His unseen, but omniscient plan. Think of a seed. As long as a seed remains in the light, it cannot develop and will never become what it was created to be. The seed must be planted in the soil, in a dark place, so that the potential on the inside will come to life. In the same way, there are seeds of greatness in us—dreams, goals, talents, potential— that will only come to life in a dark place.

6. There is Jesus.
When we relapse, and think we've gone too far.
When we cry, and can't dry our tears.
When we fall, and need someone to help us up.
When we fail, and need help trying again.
When we have a big decision, but don't know what is right.
Through all these things . . .
There is Jesus.
His grace is sweeter.
His love is greater.
His wisdom is perfect.

7. Having anxiety and depression is like being scared and tired at the same time. It's the fear of failure but no desire to be productive. It's wanting connection but being afraid of socializing. It's wanting to be alone but not wanting to be lonely.

It's caring about everything and then caring about nothing . . . sometimes within minutes or hours. It's feeling everything all at once, and then feeling paralyzingly numb. I hope this helps you understand those you come in contact with on a daily or weekly basis . . . whether they are your friends or family. And to those who go through this on a daily basis, God bless you and strengthen you. You are strong, determined, and worthy of help. Please stay. Please seek help. Please reach out to those who love you. Please take your medication, get exercise, see a therapist, get sunlight, take your vitamins/supplements, and get enough sleep.

We can end the stigma together.

8. The Red Sea was parted at the opportune moment. It happened right before Pharaoh was about to annihilate Moses and his followers. It happened right before the Israelites were about to give up. It absolutely was a miracle—but few realize that it wouldn't have happened if Moses didn't stand right up to the edge of the water beforehand. Moses had to show God he was willing to have God do "the impossible." Sometimes in life, God wants to part *our* Red Sea's, but He can't because we don't exercise the faith to step right up to the water (or take one step into it). Is there an opportunity for you to step up to the water, and allow God to part your Red Sea?

9. We don't know what the future holds . . . but we do know who holds the future.

It's been a struggle recently to try and understand what the future holds. Will it be good? Will my family be safe? Will life be sound?

But, at the end of the day, when the clouds of opposition lift and I start to experience peace—this phrase keeps coming back.

It may seem like God is taking something from you right now. It's probably something you love or cherish. You may not understand what's going on.

I get it. It's so hard. I hope that we can trust and believe that He has something greater planned . . . something to give us a longer-term peace and fulfillment than what we're experiencing now.

10. The devil's job is to rob you of your destiny. He knows you. He knows your purpose. He knows your capacity. He knows your strengths and weaknesses. And nothing makes him happier than to see you give up, give in, and stop trusting God when times get hard. He wants you to be miserable. He wants you to have nothing but regret. He wants you to look back in thirty years and say, "Oh gosh, if only I'd trusted God instead of my own strength . . ." So, right now—when all you want to do is give up—I hope you can keep holding on . . . just a little bit longer.

Don't worry about being fruitful. Just be faithful.

God is for us. God is for *you*. You're engraved upon the palms of His hands.

11. One of my favorite principles of life is this:

    God says, "You plant the seed. I'll make the tree." Amazing. We *don't* have to make the tree!

    The roots, the leaves, the compounds, the chemicals, the branches, the colors . . . not up to us! What's our responsibility? Plant.

    Plant the seed.

    Make the effort.

    Say the prayer.

    Nourish the roots.

    Read the book.

    Study the material.

    Go for a walk.

    Put in the effort.

    Just try.

    Results = In God's hands.

    Effort = In our hands.

12. Often, the most difficult place for us to be in life is God's waiting room. When we're waiting on God to fulfill a promise, heal an affliction, provide a relationship, or change a circumstance, it can be *so* hard to wait. I know there are many reading this who find themselves in similar situations. But, just as we develop increased muscle capacity by exercising, and increased mental capacity by studying, we develop increased spiritual capacity by trusting God when things don't make sense. Remember, our faith is most proven when we don't know, yet trust anyway. To my friends, your spiritual strength will be developed in the "wait rooms" of life, just as your physical strength is developed in the other "weight rooms" of life.

    Keep believing.

    Keep trusting.

    Keep hoping.

    Keep close to God who is a "very present help" in our times of need (Psalms 46:1, KJB).

13. We may not always stick with God, but God will always stick with us.

14. God's ability to work does not hinge on our perception of Him working. This has been a really hard lesson for me to continually learn. I often feel like the miracle needs to happen now in order for everything to work out smoothly. I struggle with placing my wants on hold in order to let His needs for my life take effect. Often in life, we find ourselves in the "wait rooms," and just like a "weight room" at the gym, the results don't become efficacious in our lives until the price has been paid. The price of struggle. The price of effort. The price of persistence. God is working in our lives. God is working in your life. God is working behind the scenes. He's making sure the right people are in place, the resources are there, the finances are available, the angels are standing by ready to assist, etc. It's our responsibility to hold out faithful, and continue to trust even when our perception of Him working is blurry at best. Keep going my friends. The Lord loves your effort.

15. Jesus said, "I am God, and there is none like me" (Isaiah 46:9, NLT). You may be in a desert right now with no water in sight. You're exhausted. You're hopeless. You're thirsty. You're done. You can't even begin to imagine how God could provide the resources you need to continue on. Remember today, my friends—God is God and we are not. He has the past, present, and future laid before Him at all times. He has knowledge of every resource and helpmeet for you. He is the Living Water you need in your desert right now (John 4:10) Turn to Him, and find replenishment. Turn to Him, and find strength. Turn to Him, and find life.

16. It's not your responsibility to feed the 5,000 and perform the miracle—your responsibility is to bring the 5 loaves of bread and 2 fish to Jesus . . . and then *He* feeds the 5,000 and provides the miracle. You may be in a situation right now where you need a miracle. You're overwhelmed, tired, lost, exhausted, sad, and frustrated. You don't know what you're going to do to feed your 5,000, and all you have are 5 loaves of bread and 2 fish. God says to you today, "Perfect. That's all I need. Bring me what you have, and I'll provide the miracle." It's never our responsibility to provide the miracle. It's always our responsibility to provide the effort. Whether feeding your 5,000 means going back to school, providing for your family, being a single mom or dad, battling mental or physical

illness, taking care of a loved one who is sick, dealing with grief, struggling with a faith crisis, seeking an answer to prayer, or just trying to make it one more day—Jesus understands. He's there. He loves you. He *wants* to provide the miracle for you. Simply bring Him what you have, and He'll multiply the remainder.

17. Something I've learned in life is that the devil tries to minimize sin beforehand, and tries to maximize it afterwards.

    Beforehand:

    "It's no big deal."

    "Everyone does it."

    "You can just repent after."

    "Just go for it . . . you deserve it."

    Afterward:

    "You're a failure.

    "You'll be miserable forever."

    "You're too far gone."

    "You promised you wouldn't do it again, and you did it. There's no redemption for you."

    See the pattern? Satan doesn't want us to be happy. He doesn't care about us. He doesn't want us to experience Christ's light. God, on the other hand, wants us to feel fulfilled, grateful, and filled with light. God *is* the light. Satan *is* the dark. To those who are struggling with sin and temptation:

    Keep going.

    Keep learning.

    Keep growing.

    Get back up.

    Turn to Jesus. He is the answer. He is the strength you need. You're not doing this on your own.

    Isaiah 49:16 (KJV), "Behold, I have graven thee upon the palms of my hands; thy walls are continually before me."

18. Our responsibility isn't fruitfulness . . . it's faithfulness. Once we prove faithful, Jesus provides the fruit. It's all about Him. Our job is to abide. To remain. To dwell. To cling to. To follow. Staying connected to Jesus is the most guaranteed way we can bear fruit in this life. "I am the vine; you are the branches. Whoever abides in

me and I in him, he it is that bears much fruit, for apart from me you can do nothing" (John 15:5, ESV).

19. God never promised that all things would be good in our lives. He promised that He would work "all things together for our good" in our lives (Romans 8:28). Jesus cares more about developing our character than our comfort—because He knows that's where the experience and long-term fulfillment will come from. This life is a test, and just as He was tested in all things, so we must be as well. That grief, that pain, that doubt, that anxiety, that illness, that failure, that trauma . . . it will *all* be worked together for *your* good. All you need to do is stay close to the Divine Potter.

He's sculpting you.

He's molding you.

He's perfecting you.

One step at a time, one breath at a time, one prayer at a time.

20. The decisions we make are more important than the cir-cumstances we meet. Hudson Taylor, a missionary from the 1800s, said this about God doing the impossible in our lives,

> *There are three stages to every great work of God; first it is impossible, then it is difficult, then it is done.*

You may be in the "impossible/difficult" stage right now:

- Going through a divorce with a spouse, trying to deter-mine how your future will be individually and with your children.
- Trying to navigate a financial storm that's threatening to leave you penniless.
- Grieving the loss of a loved one who was taken from this earth too soon due to illness, accident, or tragedy.
- Attempting for the 1000th time to break the addiction, habit, or action that's weighing you down.
- Whatever the circumstance is, choose Jesus.
- One of my favorite things about Him is His omnipotence, plainly stated as: "Having unlimited power." Turn your life to Him. Turn your cares to Him. Turn your sins to Him. Turn your thoughts to Him. He will help you navigate this hurricane of hurt, and this tsunami of trying times.

21. Because we're human, forgiveness is our greatest need; and because Jesus died for us, forgiveness is His greatest gift. The scripture says, "All have sinned, and come short of the glory of God" (Romans 3:23, KJV). But then here's the beautiful part: "Though your sins be as scarlet, they shall be as white as snow; though they be red like crimson, they shall be as wool" (Isaiah 1:18, KJV).

    Jesus is the Giver of Grace.

    Jesus is the Haven of Hope.

    Jesus is the Master of Mercy.

    Jesus is the Rock of Redemption.

    Whatever you've done, wherever you've been, He wants you to come home, and more importantly, He wants you to *feel* at home. Just as His arms were outstretched on the cross during His death, His arms are outstretched now during His eternal life. Come unto Jesus and be made whole.

22. When something isn't working out in your life, God is working something out in you. He's the potter, we're the clay. He's the artist, we're the canvas. He's the master, we're the apprentice. Because He created us, He has the blueprints for our lives. He knows what piece goes where. He knows when to use a hammer vs. a screwdriver vs. a paint brush vs. a pencil.

    God's timing is perfect. (Ephesians 3:1)

    God's wisdom is omniscient. (Isaiah 46:9–10)

    He's working it out for you right now. He's putting the pieces in place. He's bringing the people together. He's providing the resources. He who "never slumbers or sleeps" (Psalm 121:4, NLT) is working out in you a marvelous masterpiece, and when it is done, as Job of old said, "[You] shall come forth as gold" (Job 23:10, KJV).

23. Wherever you are in your faith journey—He's going to help you through. Wherever you are in your wilderness wanderings—He's going to help you through. Wherever you are in your financially uncertainty—He's going to help you through. Wherever you are in your physical or mental or emotional recovery—He's going to help you through. The scriptures say that God is a "very present help" in times of trouble (Psalms 46:1, ESV). Not a "casually present" or a "maybe if I have time" or a "only if I feel like it" or "but I helped you with that yesterday" type of help. He's a *very present* help. He's

there. He's present. He's always available. And just like He lifted up Peter when he sank in the sea and gave him a hug, He'll lift you up too. Put your hand in His, and trust His grace to help you through your storm.

24. There's never been a better time in your life than right now to start doing what God has asked you to do, and living the life God has created you to live.

I repeat again the scripture I used at the end of chapter 11,

Who shall separate us from the love of Christ? Shall tribulation, or distress, or persecution, or famine, or nakedness, or danger, or sword? . . . Nay, in all these things we are more than conquerors through him that loved us. For I am persuaded, that neither death, nor life, nor angels, nor principalities, nor powers, nor things present, nor things to come, nor height, nor depth, nor any other creature, shall be able to separate us from the love of God, which is in Christ Jesus our Lord. (Romans 8:35, 37–39, KJV).

Your failures won't separate you from the love of Christ.

Your sins won't separate you from the love of Christ.

Your mistakes won't separate you from the love of Christ.

Your temptations won't separate you from the love of Christ.

Your past won't separate you from the love of Christ.

Your sorrows won't separate you from the love of Christ.

Your insecurities won't separate you from the love of Christ.

Your secrets that are too personal to share with any other living soul won't separate you from the love of Christ.

Through it all, He's with us.

Through it all, He counsels us.

Through it all, He is good, kind, righteous, powerful, wise, and forgiving.

He won't lead us astray. That is a promise.

Go forward, friends. I believe in you. He believes in you. You have not come this far to only come this far.

Your Wonderful Counselor is here to take you the rest of the way.

I thank God that whenever we wish, we can look up from our infirmity, reach out for His hand, and seek His guidance in our lives.

Endnote Citations

1 "Wonderful," *Google English Dictionary*.

2 "Counselor," *Google English Dictionary*.

3 Miller, Kelly, "27 Scientifically Proven Benefits of Counseling," *Positive Psychology.com*, 14 Jan. 2020, https://positivepsychology.com/benefits-of-counseling/.

4 "A Quote by Mark Twain," *Goodreads*, Accessed June 24, 2023, https://www.goodreads.com/quotes/308159-worrying-is-like-paying-a-debt-you-don-t-owe.

5 "A Quote by Mark Twain," *Goodreads*, Accessed June 24, 2023, https://www.goodreads.com/quotes/31860-i-ve-lived-through-some-terrible-things-in-my-life-some.

6 Carnegie, Dale, *How to stop worrying and start living* (New York: Simon and Schuster, 1984).

7 Newman, John Henry, "Lead Kindly Light," 1833.

8 Carnegie, Dale, *How to Stop Worrying and Start Living* (Simon and Schuster, 1948).

9 Warren, Rick qtd. in Above Inspiration, "Let Go & Trust God | Overcoming Worry - Inspirational & Motivational Video," *YouTube*, 17 Jun. 2019, https://www.youtube.com/watch?v=jou5ANZX1BQ.

10 Austin, Lynn, Candle in the Darkness (Baker Publishing Group, 2002), 179.

11 Barton, Ruth Haley, *Invitation to Solitude and Silence* (InterVarsity Press, 2004), 49.

12 Sandomir, Richard, "Victoria Ruvolo, Who Forgave Her Attacker, Is Dead at 59," *New York Times*, 28 Mar. 2019, https://www.nytimes.com/2019/03/28/obituaries/victoria-ruvolo-dead.html.

13 "Patient," *Merriam-Webster.com*, https://www.merriam-webster.com/dictionary/patient.

14 Fairchild, Mary. "The Sin of Pride According to the Bible." *Learn Religions*. 28 Oct. 2020. https://www.learnreligions.com/the-sin-of-pride-according-to-the-bible-5080290.

15 Spurgeon, Charles Haddon. "On Humbling Ourselves Before God." *The Spurgeon Center*. 1 Jan. 1970. https://www.spurgeon.org/resource-library/sermons/on-humbling-ourselves-before-god.

16 Ramos, Liz. "Rape Survivor and former human trafficker learns to love again through recovery." *Columbia Missourian*. 27 Jan. 2016. https://www.columbiamissourian.com/news/local/rape-survivor-and-former-human-trafficker-learns-to-love-again-through-recovery/article_de80da48-c56c-11e5-b3da-531ad967b179.html.

17 FaithPot Positive Stories. "Cab Driver Takes Dying Elderly Woman For A

Ride And Her Story Leaves Him Speechless." *FaithPot*. 29 July 2021. https://www.faithpot.com/cab-driver-inspirational-story/.

18 Coley, Rebekah Levine, and Christopher F. Baum. "Redacted: Trends in mental health symptoms, service use, and unmet need for services among U.S. adults through the first 9 months of the COVID-19 pandemic." *Translational Behavioral Medicine*. Vol. 11, Issue 10, Oct. 2021, pages 1947–1956. https://doi.org/10.1093/tbm/ibab030.

19 Hall, Travis, "Discovering Your Purpose," *Cultivate*, 23 Nov. 2020, https://cultivatemypurpose.com/discovering-your-purpose/.

20 Bednar, David A. "The Character of Christ." Brigham Young University-Idaho Religion Symposium. 25 Jan. 2003. https://www2.byui.edu/Presentations/Transcripts/ReligionSymposium/2003_01_25_Bednar.htm.

21 C.S. Lewis, Mere Christianity (HarperCollins, 2001), 142.

22 Ezra Taft Benson, "Jesus Christ—Gifts and Expectations," *Ensign*, Dec. 1988, 4, churchofjesuschrist.org.

23 Larry Y. Wilson, "The Savior's Message of Repentance," *Ensign*, Feb. 2016, 48, churchofjesuschrist.org.

24 Russell M. Nelson, "Four Gifts That Jesus Christ Offers to You," First Presidency Christmas Devotional, Dec. 2018, churchofjesuschrist.org.

25 Luther, Martin, *Collected works of Martin Luther: Martin Luther's large catechism, concerning Christian Liberty, the Smalcald Articles and Martin Luther's 95 these*. (Charleston: Bibliobazaar, 2007).

26 Egay, Francesca. "The Most Touching Story on Peace," *Inspirationalife*, 6 Jan. 2023, https://inspirationalife.com/the-most-touching-story-on-peace/.

27 David A. Bednar, "That We Might 'Not . . . Shrink' (D&C 19:18)," CES Devotional for Young Adults, University of Texas Arlington, 3 Mar. 2013, churchofjesuschrist.org.

Bible Translation Guide

BSB	Berean Standard Bible
ERV	English Revised Version
ESV	English Standard Version
KJV	King James Version
NASB	New American Standard Bible
NHEB	New Heart English Bible
NIV	New International Version
NKJV	New King James Version
NLT	New Living Translation

About the Author

Drew Young is a native of the east coast, growing up in Connecticut, and now resides in Texas with his wife and two daughters. His first book published in 2020, *The Meaning of Your Mission: Lessons and Principles to Know You Are Enough*, debuted as a #1 LDS bestseller on Amazon and continues to help individuals understand their worth and overcome perfectionism. In addition, his second book, *Stand Guard at the Door of Your Mind*, released August of 2021 and climbed to #1 emotional success bestseller on Amazon and helps people increase their mental wellness.

Drew is a certified professional coach and works to help individuals increase their mental wellness, overcome perfectionism/anxious tendencies, improve their scholastic/professional performance, promote positive mindsets in their lives, and recover from habitual drug use.

Drew loves Jesus and sharing His light and hopes that those who follow him on social media will also find strength, hope, and peace.

To get in touch with Drew, find him on Instagram or Facebook, or send him an email at youngbandrew@gmail.com.